S0-EFM-567

78.865

Nederland as it looked in 1899

# NederLanD

## A TRIP TO CLOUDLAND

### ISABEL M. BECKER

**NEDERLAND — A TRIP TO CLOUDLAND**

First Edition

Copyright 1989 by Isabel M. Becker

All rights reserved. No part of this publication may be reproduced or transmitted in any form or means, electronic or mechanical, including photocopying, recording, or use of any information storage and retrieval system, without permission in writing from the publisher.

Published and distributed by Scott Becker Press, P.O. Box 501, Denver, CO 80201

ISBN 0-945743-13-0

Printed and bound in the United States of America.

This first edition of the Nederland book was printed on a Heidelberg 4-color GTO perfector press by Richard J. Shorey and James K. Cinnamon at Special Techniques, Denver, Colorado. The German Heidelberg press produces the most exacting and accurate offset printing possible today. Some of the imagery in the book shows detail finer than three hundred lines per inch. The press produces accuracy and register better than one one-thousandth of an inch and can print four colors on both sides of a piece of paper within one pass through the press.

The Nederland book is printed on S.D. Warren Number One Coated Lustro Dull Enamel. Color separations were obtained electronically from a laser scanner and 175 line duotones from Kodak Ultratec film through an elliptical dot screen.

# CONTENTS

# FOREWORD

In the 1920s, when Isabel Becker was a child, her parents fell in love with Nederland and made it their summer home. It's only appropriate that Isabel felt compelled to write **NEDERLAND, A TRIP TO CLOUDLAND.**

This book, however, is not a collection of childhood memories. In fact, the author says very little about herself in favor of providing well-researched history on an unusual Boulder County mining town. Located on the crossroads of Boulder Canyon and the old Black Hawk-Ward wagon road (used to transport mining supplies between these two gold mining and milling centers), Nederland became known as a freighting center. More importantly, it grew and thrived because of three types of mining —silver, gold and tungsten.

The Trip to Cloudland in the book's title refers to a promotional phrase from brochures of the somewhat elusive Switzerland Trail of America. Nederland's past is intertwined with this narrow-gauge railroad even though it never formally stopped there. The closest station and freight depot was at Cardinal, although during the construction of Barker Dam, a temporary spur line was run through Nederland from Sulfide Flats, just east of Eldora. During low water, the railroad grade, like a ghost from the past, reappears from the bottom of the Reservoir.

Longtime residents as well as first time visitors will find something new in **NEDERLAND, A TRIP TO CLOUDLAND.** Much needed, it fills a gap in regional history.

**Silvia Pettem**
Author and historian

Boulder Canyon

# BOULDER CANYON

## 1

From Boulder city limits, a drive up the canyon to Barker
Dam takes less than 30 minutes these days. In the 1920s,
the drive in my dad's Model T Ford took considerably more
than an hour. Usually the radiator boiled over somewhere in
the vicinity of Boulder Falls. This meant a stop, a climb
down to the creek for water, then a wait until the "T" was
cool enough to go on. The highway in 1920 was a full two-
way road built by convicts from the Colorado State
Penitentiary and a great improvement over the one-way
wagon road that preceded it.

That famous wagon road of 1871 — can anyone imagine
what it was like? Can anyone imagine Boulder Canyon in its
natural state? Steep and narrow, huge boulders in the
stream bed, rock cliffs rising straight up out of the water in
places, and one nearly impassable stretch above the falls
appropriately named "The Narrows" — the canyon
presented formidable obstacles. Even to hike through the
canyon was an arduous undertaking, but Boulderites were

determined to build a road to the rich mines in the mountains.

The first few miles of road in Boulder Canyon were built in 1865 as part of a wagon road to Central City. James Maxwell and Clinton Tyler, Boulder financiers, organized The Boulder Valley and Central City Wagon Road Company. On February 8, 1865, they were granted permission to build.

In three months, the road reached Orodell, a settlement at the junction of Boulder Canyon and Four Mile Canyon. Two miles beyond Orodell, where the lower part of Magnolia Hill enters Boulder Canyon from the south, the route left Boulder Canyon. It went up Magnolia Hill, over to South Boulder Creek and joined the Enterprise Road into Blackhawk.

Six years later, because of the rush to Caribou and its phenomenal silver mine, the canyon road from Magnolia Hill to Nederland was built. Four Boulder men (John F. Buttles, Amos Widner, Anthony Arnett and William Pound) organized a second wagon road company to finish the direct route from Boulder to Nederland. The Boulder Canyon Wagon Road opened on May 20, 1871.

The road was a major accomplishment, an amazing piece of construction. Huge boulders and timbers were used for support in some places. Where rock cliffs rising from the creek channel were encountered, a bridge was built to the other side, or a log cribwork (filled with earth and rocks) was constructed around the base of the cliff.

The finished road — narrow, steep and hazardous — crossed from one side of the canyon to the other over 33 bridges. Today's modern highway is so greatly changed, only the keen observer would notice whether it crossed the stream at all.

The dusty one-way wagon road was a toll road that never did pay back the men who built it. Constant upkeep took every cent of the toll-gate revenue. But it wasn't disappointing to Boulder men who financed it; the road gave Boulder part of the trade which formerly had gone to Denver via Clear Creek Canyon.

The road delighted tourists too; they were enthused about scenic places such as Boulder Falls, Perfect Tree and Castle Rock. A horse-drawn vehicle called the Tallyho, an open-top wagon that could carry some 10 or 12 passengers, was a popular vehicle for sightseeing. Tallyho traveling was leisurely. Meandering along a winding road near the floor of the canyon, tourists could enjoy the sights and sounds of Boulder Canyon — the intriguingly shaped rocks which they named, the wildlife and the sounds of rushing Boulder Creek as they crossed primitive wooden bridges.

Some of the favorite old scenic points no longer exist in their original state, and with highway improvements, some are hidden from view. Other old landmarks are still highly visible. One of the first in lower Boulder Canyon is the 75-year-old Public Service plant, down along the creek just east of the tunnel entrance. This power plant is a major part of the Boulder hydroelectric system.

Another noticeable feature is a rock retaining wall high on Magnolia Hill. This wall supports the steep road of 1865, now Boulder County Highway No. 132 leading to the little town, Magnolia. On the south side of Boulder Creek and just west of El Vado Motel, the retaining wall can easily be seen.

Boulder Falls is considered the halfway point in the canyon where the waters of North Boulder Creek spill over a high rocky ledge to join Middle Boulder Creek in the canyon. Early travelers loved to picnic near the falls and enjoyed the perfection of its mountain atmosphere. This miniature shangri-la environment is not visible from the highway but is found only a mere 100 paces off the road. A 35-foot thunderous waterfall descends into an enchanting cove surrounded by woods and rock formations. Today people still picnic there, and almost everyone enjoys the soothing mental atmosphere created by sounds of the waterfall.

Castle Rock, a huge serrated mass of black rock rising 300 feet above the canyon floor, attracts professional rock climbers as well as many less-experienced climbers who seek challenge and excitement. Both Castle Rock and the Public Service plant are places where you can see and drive over a section of the old convict-built road just by taking a short detour off the main highway.

Today's modern thoroughfare through Boulder Canyon was more than 10 years in the making. Rebuilding started in 1941. The first part finished, a stretch of road slightly less than one mile in length, was the steep hill between Barker Dam and Tungsten. Work ceased during the years of the Second World War. Following the war, the reservoir section from the dam to Nederland was built. The highway below Tungsten took shape in five succeeding stages. Boulder Canyon highway tunnel, cut through solid rock and eliminating a dangerous curve, was opened to traffic on January 8, 1953. Finally, in 1955 the road was completed to Boulder city limits. Built by the State Bureau of Public Roads, the project including recreational facilities cost $2.38 million. It takes travelers to the little-known mining town called Nederland.

Tourists in Boulder Canyon

Arrow points to still visible letters, CCPCo, the old trade letters for Central Colorado Power Company, predecessor of Public Service.

Boulder Falls

The Narrows

Castle Rock

Perfect Tree was famous for decades, a majestic blue spruce, 83 feet tall, remarkable for its dense branches that tapered symmetrically from base to tip. Foresters estimated its age at 300 years. Rose Jackson, who lives in Tungsten, said, "Perfect Tree was still there in 1962 when I visited Boulder Canyon. I remember stopping to read the sign."

Today, its location requires a search, for the tree is gray and dead, not as easy to recognize as the magnificent living tree of earlier days. But Perfect Tree still stands on the stream bank about a mile below Castle Rock. "Age and budworm infestation caused it to die," said Allan Rogers whose family owns the land where Perfect Tree stands. "Deterioration of the tree occurred in just the last three or four years," declared Rogers. According to his estimate, the tree would be between 375 and 400 years old.

# NEDERLAND

## 2

Nederland in its earliest stage was just a cluster of small cabins called Dayton. The first addition to this settlement was a two-story ranch house built of logs, known to pioneers as Brown's Mountain House.

Nathan W. Brown, the first homesteader, may have come to the community as early as 1850. Brown built a fine cabin on a 40-acre tract of rich meadowland which became famous as an inn. His location was a natural stopping point for hunters and prospectors of the day. Because of the inn, the place was called Brownsville as well as Dayton until 1871 when a post office was established, and Nederland-to-be was renamed Middle Boulder.

The year 1871 brought the first big change to Middle Boulder — the building of a mill. Cincinnati businessman Abel Breed acquired ownership of the Caribou Mine, four miles to the west, and needed to relocate his milling operations from Caribou Hill to the milder climate of Middle Boulder.

Many mills and concentration works in Colorado were built without sufficient study of the ores to be handled, and they were doomed to failure. The Breed and Cutter Reduction Works (later called the Caribou Mill) was extraordinary; it was a success from the beginning. Abel Breed built his mill, terracing it in five floors for gravity-flow ore handling. At the upper end was a crusher and three automatic feeders. The next floor down had 15 stamps for dry crushing and pulverizing. Four cylinders on the next level revolved slowly while ore was roasted and chlorodized. On the next terrace, ore was placed in pans of quicksilver and kept in motion until amalgamated. In the melting room on the fifth level, silver was cast into bars.

Near the mill, other buildings were constructed — a fully equipped assay office, a weighing office, a company office, a residence building, a few storage buildings, outhouses and a stable. Construction of the Caribou Mill marked the real founding of Middle Boulder. Small town businesses supporting the new milling industry quickly sprang up. Many homes were built, and Middle Boulder's population rose to 200. Boulder Canyon Wagon Road was finished the same year — 1871. Middle Boulder was then on two main roads: one already existing which ran northward from Blackhawk to Ward and Estes Park; the other a new road coming up Boulder Canyon and crossing the north-south road on its way to Caribou.

The great wealth of the Caribou Mine was promoted in

national fairs and exhibits. Foreign investors, mining engineers and metallurgists became interested as well as eastern U.S. mining men and investors. When U.S. President Ulysses S. Grant and his wife made a visit to Central City on April 28, 1873, bars of Caribou silver were laid in front of the Teller House entrance. The president and his party stepped from their carriage and walked into the hotel across this silver-paved entrance. The **Daily Central City Register** for April 29, 1873, reports the president was "quite incredulous when told that the slabs were genuine silver, but finally had to accept the truth."

This great publicity stunt brought fame not only to the Caribou Mine but also to Nederland's mill where the silver bars were cast. Later in the year, Breed sold the Caribou Mine and mill property to the Mining Company Nederland of Holland for $3 million.

From the time of the Dutch company's ownership of the Caribou properties, the mill site was referred to as "the Netherlands," which meant "lower lands." Both mill and mine were located in high altitudes — the mill at 8,237 feet and the mine at nearly 10,000 feet. Compared to the mine, the mill was on lower land. Some of the mining men from Holland lived in Middle Boulder hotels during the years of their ownership, and as "the Netherlands" was heard, it was finally accepted. When the town was incorporated in 1875, "Nederland" became its official name.

Unemployment depressed both Caribou and Nederland in 1876 after the financial collapse of the Mining Company Nederland. Sold at a sheriff's sale and reorganized under new management, the Caribou Mine continued full-scale operations for another seven years. The great Caribou closed for the first time on January 1, 1883, and from that day gradually sank into decline. From time to time the Caribou Mill ceased its activity, being dependent on the mine, but business in Nederland never stopped completely. The town gradually attained its own importance as a shipping center and distribution point, as well as a famous tungsten mining center.

In 1889 only seven families lived in Nederland, but from that low point, the town began to revive. Nederland struggled through some lean years until gold was discovered at Eldora.

By 1897, due to gold mining, Nederland's population rose to 200, and the next year it rose again — to approximately 500. But the gold boom at Eldora lasted only a few years. As mining activity diminished, Nederland's population shrunk. By the turn of the century, residents in Nederland again numbered about 200.

Caribou in 1900, once a proud and famous little town, was vanishing — population 44.

Brown's mountain house and mill at Nederland

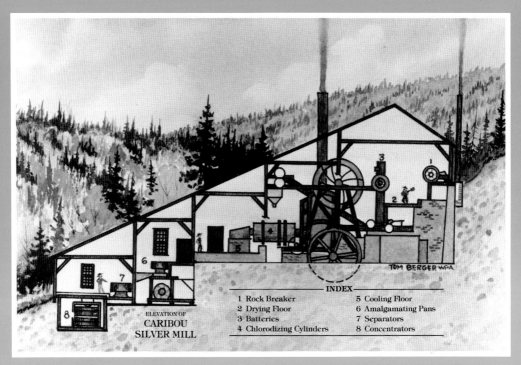

INDEX

| | |
|---|---|
| 1 Rock Breaker | 5 Cooling Floor |
| 2 Drying Floor | 6 Amalgamating Pans |
| 3 Batteries | 7 Separators |
| 4 Chlorodizing Cylinders | 8 Concentrators |

ELEVATION OF
CARIBOU
SILVER MILL

TOM BERGER WPA

The external dimensions of the Caribou Mill are 100 feet in width and 165 feet in length. There are five terraces of floors, devoted to as many different degrees in the treatment of ores. The first or upper floor, upon which rests a Blake crusher, (1) is the Ore room, where the wagons deposit the silver rock. It is then passed through the crusher and into the kiln. From the kiln it goes to the fifteen stamp battery, and (3) is there ground to powder beneath ponderous iron pestles, weighing seven hundred and fifty pounds each, dropping eight and a half inches and one hundred times per minute. After leaving the battery it passes through a number forty wire sieve, or bolt cloth, and by conveyors to the hoppers resting over the Bruckner furnaces (4) awaiting to receive the glittering dust. These great cylindrical furnaces have a capacity of two tons each every eight hours, or a ton for each of the twenty-four hours. From the furnace it falls red hot into an iron car resting on iron rails beneath, and at each round a charge from a single furnace, until the four are empty, is then wheeled a few feet and dumped and spread on the cooling floor, (5) where it is wet down or sprinkled with water, and left to become cool. In the amalgamating pans (6) the dusty treasure next finds a lodgement. These pans are ten in number, each with a capacity of one thousand pounds to the charge. In the pans quick silver is introduced, which collects to itself the genuine silver, after which it is drawn off and strained, thus separating and saving both. The remaining contents of the pans are then let into five settlers, (7) that catch any particles of silver or quick-silver that may have escaped the pans; and to guard against accidents. In the basement are two agitators, (8) each of which receives separately the entire contents of the five settlers through which the base material passes on its way to the creek. Thus it will be seen no loss can be sustained.

Professor Dawley, the superintendent in charge of the mill, has so far perfected the system of reducing the ore, that the tailings after leaving the agitators will not assay $5 a ton. After the amalgam is taken from the pans and strained it is submitted to a retort, (9) when the remainder of the quick is sublimed or vaporized, and the silver then becomes crude bullion. It is next submitted to plumbage crucibles and placed in the melting furnace (10) where it becomes molten silver, after which it is poured into cast iron moulds — brick shape, and out of them comes silver bricks weighing from eighteen hundred to two thousand ounces each. These bricks are then taken to the assay office and there assayed and marked, which renders them ready for shipment; 850 fine is their usual average, but some lots run as high as 950. These works are styled the old Freiberg process of calcining and amalgamating. The mill is built on the Nevada style, and in all its details for treating these ores. It is as near perfect as such works can well be made. All this extensive and ponderous machinery is driven by an engine of one hundred and fifty horsepower. From eight to twelve percent of salt is used, or about three thousand five hundred pounds every twenty-four hours. The labour of twenty men is required in and about the mill to keep it in operation day and night.

Crushing, drying, sorting and sacking of ore

A.D. Breed Reduction Works in Caribou showing nearness of the Continental Divide

These are the famous silver bricks President Grant trod on in Central City. Weighing approximately 70 pounds each and measuring about 13 inches long by 4 inches high and 4 inches wide, they were cast into bars at Nederland in the Breed and Cutter Mill. The silver came from ores of the Caribou Mine.

Early Nederland and casting silver bricks

BROWN

NATHANIEL W.
DIED DEC. 28, 1898

VIRGINIA J.
DIED FEB. 4, 1917

Nathan Brown's name survives on this marker in the town cemetery.

Rose Northrop of Boulder donated the William S. Smith painting of Caribou to the Carnegie Branch Library for Local History in Boulder where it hangs today.

## CARIBOU, AS IT APPEARED IN THE YEAR 1904

By William S. Smith

There are 85 numbered items in the painting which include homes, people, mines, mountain peaks, train, horses, cattle, 5 working mines (those with smoke coming from their chimneys), non-working mines which had closed down prior to 1904, etc.

This work is of the entire town of Caribou as it appeared in 1904 after the disastrous fire of 1879 had destroyed a large portion of it. The fire of 1905-06 started in the Billy Donald Hotel and destroyed a number of buildings, Numbers 27, 16, 15, 14, 13, 12, 11, 10, 6, and 2.

Note that the picture shows ricks filled with three-foot lengths of cord wood at the side of each house. Each building had pole props on the east side to help them withstand the strong winds that blew continually.

**1 — School House**

Charlie, Bill, and Dan Smith attended school in this one-room building. Charlie was in the fourth grade, Bill third and Dan in first. Our cousins, Sammie and May Robertson, also attended at the same time. School was in session only three months during the summer (June 1 to August 31) because of the severity of the weather the rest of the year.

Miss Allen (#21) was our teacher. She is pictured in front of the school attempting to frighten a bull away. Miss Black also taught here for a time. Children playing ball are the three Smith boys and Gene Trollope. See #23. Grace and Sadie Miller are shown at the rear of the schoolhouse. The team of horses nearby (named Bill and Dan) belonged to Grandpa Bennett (#22). Along with his other possessions, these horses were traded off by his son, Uncle John Bennett, after the death of Grandpa.

**2 — Grandpa Bennett's House**

Painted as it appeared in 1903-04. It was torn down by Uncle John Bennett who used the lumber to erect a house in Nederland. He used a team and wagon to transport it to Nederland. It was here that Grandpa died January 19, 1905. He is buried on the west side (in about the center) of the Nederland cemetery beside his second wife, Mary Florence, who had passed away at the old ranch below Tungsten on February 10, 1885. She died on the same day that she gave birth to Aunt Florence. The double tombstone was handmade by Uncle John Bennett. The inscription includes a record of history hollowed out of one side of the stone. Uncle John disposed of Grandpa's team that year along with the 45 revolver, the Winchester Rifle and many other items.

**3 — Jim Buttler House**

This house was one in which I, William Smith, was born August 22, 1897. It was the only Caribou house still standing in 1967, so you might say that I was born in the last Caribou house to fall. In 1971 Betty and Gordon Wickstrom, my daughter and son-in-law picked up two of the window sill boards from this house and had them made into a frame for a painting of flatiron that I had done for them. That same year in which I was born (1897) our grandmother from Chicago (Father's mother) came to visit us. Three of her sons were at Caribou at the time — our father, Uncle Sam, and Uncle Bill. The uncles were operating the Gold Leaf Mine. It was located just north of Hessie on the south edge of the Caribou Flats. Grandma became ill due to the altitude of nearly 10,000 feet and was able to stay only a few days.

**4 — Our House** (John G. and Mary Jane Smith)

Purchased for taxes in 1902. Born in this house were two of my brothers: Henry Pritchard Smith, January 4, 1904, and Hugh Boyd Smith, February 12, 1906.

**5 — Dave Boles House**

**6 — Stafford House**

**7 — Ed Aller and John Nusom House**

They operated the Silver Point Mine (#35).

**8 — Boarding House**

Mamie and Gertie Miller were the proprietors and were in competition with the Cap Trollope Hotel (#14). Also see #32.

**9 — McKenzie House**

Horse and buggie pictured in the yard.

**10 — Rental House**

Different tenants lived here for short intervals of time.

**11 — Mrs. DeBornfine's House**

She was Mrs. Trollope's sister.

**12 — Caribou Church**

Built in 1875 and was erected between a house and a saloon.

**13 — Pete Werley's Saloon**

**14 — Trollope Hotel**

Housed as many as thirty miners both summers and winters for $30 per month which included both board and room. Hotel burned March 1905.

**15 — Jim Greer Grocery and Clothing Store**

Burned at the same time as did the other Potosi Street buildings. Mr. Greer then operated a store in #34 building from that time until his death in 1909. Sometime after this, this building also burned.

**16 — Storage Buildings**

Three small buildings used for storage. The one on stilts was an assay office for sampling ore. Used 1894 to 1899.

**17 — Sherman House or Sherman Hotel**

Also known as the Uncle Billy Donald Hotel. It was a large, three-story building. Operated by Cap Trollope when he first came to Caribou.

**18 — Old Foundation**

We children played many happy hours here.

**19 — Wagon**

Wally Hinman was driver of wagon loaded with cord wood destined for the St. Louis Gold Mine which was located a short distance north and east of the Caribou Cemetery. This mine had a tramway to carry ore down 1500 feet to the Mill located at the west end of Coon Trail canyon on the north side and against the base of Idaho Mountain. This ountain runs from the cemetery to the Boulder County Tunnel at New Cardinal. Coon Trail valley extends all the way from Caribou to Nederland.

**20 — Potosi Silver Mine Dump**

**21 — Cattle**

Frequently cattle would wade through the swamps and enter the town. They craved salt which was not included in their diet at that time. They not only soiled the yards but even entered the houses. They would frighten the pupils at school and sometimes even the teachers (#1). There were a few instances in which the wandering cows ate the miners' dynamite which caused them to bloat and die.

**22 — Grandpa Bennett's Team and Wagon**

Painted near the school. Mentioned in #1.

**23 — Children at School**

Mentioned in #1.

**24 — Rover, the Smith dog**

Chasing cattle from our yard at the command of Mother.

**25 — Barns**

Smaller ones used by Grandpa. Larger red barn, which stood in front of our house #4, belonged to Wally Hinman and was his main barn. Here freighters would lodge their horses overnight after the long haul from Boulder. The following day they would make the return trip loaded with ore for Boulder or the Switzerland Narrow Gauge Railroad at New Cardinal.

**26 — Pete J. Werley's House**

Rented for a few months by my parents in 1902 after our trip to Missouri.

**27 — Barn**

Belonged to Cap Trollope. He kept his Brindle cow here #81. She not only gave milk used at the Hotel but was prized because she bore twin calves every two years.

**28 — Bingley House**

Mrs. Bingley was a good friend and a great help to Mother when Hugh was born in 1906. Mr. Bingley worked at the Eagle Bird Mine #37 and their daughter, Eva, attended school with us.

**29 — Rufus Gray House**

Mrs. Mollie Gray was a member of the School Board as was Cap Trollope and our father, John G. Smith. Rufus mined at Caribou and also at Central City for the greater part of his life. He and his wife are buried in the southeast corner of Green Mountain Cemetery.

**30 — Carlyle House**

Mr. Carlyle was suffering from asthma and came to Caribou for that reason. He remained there until his death which occurred a few years after we had left.

**31 — Leo Donnelly House**

He was an elderly gentleman who led the prayers at funerals. At an earlier time he operated a store in Caribou. One book states that he first established his grocery store in a tent and later moved to a frame structure.

**32 — Walt Miller House**

Mr. Miller and his three children, Sadie, Grace and Roy, resided here after the death of their mother who had been his second wife. He was the father of two daughters from his first marriage, Mamie and Gertie, who at that time operated the little boarding house located on Caribou Hill (#8).

**33 — Todd House**

Little house where one of the Todd brothers lived at one time.

**34 — Store**

Jim Greer moved into this good sized building with his store wares after his first store was destroyed in the fire of 1905-06. He remained at this location until his death in 1912. John Hiney then managed it until his death in 1919. After that time Caribou was without both the post office and grocery store. It was interesting to me that Mr. Greer was a Canadian and Mr. Hiney was Swiss origin.

**35 — Silver Point Silver Mine**

This mine was located 100 feet southeast of the Black Monster Mine (#47) in the painting. Picture shows John Nusom dumping rock or muck. This mine shaft is located about 75 feet over the top of the hill on the down slope, to the left of the road to the peat bog (#47), the North Western Silver Mine (#54), and the Pandora Mine (#55). It is now the site of a tourist summer camp.

**36 — Heading House**

Virgie Heading was just about my age and I remember her well.

**37 — Eagle Bird Mine**

Silver and some gold mined here. Picture shows Harry Groves chopping wood for the steam boiler east of the shaft house. He was the hoist engineer and operated the mine. Charlie, Gene Trollope, and I used to pretend we were hoist engineers. We made hoists by using string and discarded alarm clocks with spools of thread attached to them. We would then "hoist" a nail up and down any pipe that was handy.

**38 — Baker House**

He was the owner of this house and another (#62) where he worked his mining claims.

**39 — Miners**

Miners shown on the way to the Trollope House (#14) from the Eagle Bird Mine.

**40 — Water Supply**

Caribou spring and main water supply at the time. The water came from an old tunnel which lay under the North Idaho Mountain. The people sometimes used shoulder yokes to which pails were attached to carry water to their homes. See #75, #76, and #77. Horses were watered here in a trough which John Hiney hewed out of a huge spruce log (#81).

**41 — Steam Boiler**

John Hiney transporting a four-ton steam boiler to the St. Louis Mine. It was all six horses could manage to tug it up the steep grade of the old mountain roads. Sometimes it was necessary to attach two additional horses on a push-pole behind the load to enable the feat to be accomplished.

**42 — Foundation**

Remains of the Joe Lloyd General Store which was built in the 1870's.

**43 — Old Foundation**

Remains of the Leo Donnelly Store. This was rebuilt in 1928 as a rooming and boarding house used by miners who were in the process of working over the dumps of the Potosi and the other silver mine dumps of the area. This building burned in the 1930's.

**44 — Sears and Werley Billiard Hall**

Two-story building with offices on the second floor.

**45 — Ditch**

Water in this ditch ran from springs and melting snow. Just south of our house (#4) we children built dams in which we sailed our boats. It was great fun but often we were punished for getting our shoes wet.

**46 — Caribou Mine**

Not in operation when we lived at Caribou. It ceased to operate in 1893 when the price of silver dropped and silver mining in Colorado came to a standstill. This was the best mine of the area and one of the greatest in Colorado. It produced between six and eight million dollars worth of silver and gold. It was discovered by Sam Conger in 1868.

**47 — Black Monster Mine**

See #35. This mine was discovered by Grandpa Bennett and Uncle John in 1884. As I remember the story, they sold it for $17,000 and used the money to purchase land in Boulder from Mr. Brierley which was located between Fourth and Spruce and Third and Pearl. I worked for many years at the Boulder City Garage which was located on this Third and Pearl location. They built two houses on this land that are still standing. Milt Tische, former Clerk and Recorder, resided in one of them for many years. The house has been altered many times but the 45-degree pitch of the roof can still be seen. This was the popular pitch of that time. There is a question as to how much land Grandpa owned there. He did have a large garden plot and had space on which he kept his wagon and two mules.

**48 — John Hiney House**

**49 — Peddler Wagon**

Carried and sold meat, fresh vegetables, fruit, etc., to the residents of the mining camps.

**50 — Colorado National Mine Shaft**

Silver then ran 57 oz. to the ton was discovered in this 20 foot shaft by Dad and Steve Corfield of Denver. It was located at the foot of the "Horseshoe" west of Caribou. The "X" in the painting shows the location of this silver vein. However, the last charge of explosive they used opened up a water vein which caused it to flood. They had to abandon it but with the hope of being able to return at a later date with an engine and pump and try again. That day never came. The Red Cross Tunnel is to the southeast of the Wolf Tongue Tunnel. In 1955 Anna and I, along with Verna and Elvin, drove over to that tunnel and climbed past it to the Wolf Tongue. At that time there was an old car engine hoist and cable there. The tunnel has caved in since then and buried them. We were pressed for time so did not get over to the Horse Shoe National where Dad and Steve had to tunnel through, and timber, a snowbank that never melted. This was the only way they could reach their silver vein shaft.

**51 — Wigwam Silver Mine**

The last place in Caribou where Dad mined. He worked here in 1907 just prior to the time we left to go to Eastonville, Colorado.

**52 — Poorman Mine**

Not in operation when we were in Caribou. Discovered by George Lytle in 1869. It was only 70 feet deep and the vein paralleled that of the Caribou. In one book it states that when he discovered it, he said, "Since I am a poor man, that will be the name of my claim."

**53 — Belcher Mine**

Not in operation when we were in Caribou. Closed down in 1893, as did other silver mines Colorado when the price of silver dropped.

**54 — North Western Silver Mine**

Dad worked in this mine as he did also at the Silver Point, Eagle Bird and at the Wolf Tongue.

**55 — Pandora Mine**

Operated by Jim Butler who married our last Caribou teacher, Miss Allen. He used the money he made at the Pandora Mine to buy a dairy farm near Los Angeles, California. Mother and Mrs. Butler corresponded for several years.

**56 — Buchanan Peaks**

Pictured in the extreme northeast corner of painting. The Peaks are near Ward, Colorado, area.

**57 — North Arapahoe Peaks**

**58 — Indian Peaks, Hellhole Country, and Lindberg Peak**

**59 — South Arapahoe Peaks**

We enjoyed trout carried by horseback packed in bags of green grass by Dad and Grandpa when they returned from fishing at Strawberry Creek at Middle Park. They rode the trail from the Red Cross Tunnel that ran southwest up over Bald Mountain past the South Arapahoe Peaks and on to Middle Park.

**60 — Moffat Railroad Freight Train**

Painting shows the train going over Rollins Pass winding up James Peak to the snow sheds. I painted it as it appeared to us as we stood on Goat Rock or Caribou Hill in the summer. In winter it was a spectacle to behold with its snow plough out in front blowing snow in a great fountain over the side of the mountain. We used to imagine that we could feel the ground shake. The four big engines sounded like cannons away over there on the snow-covered mountains in the still air of a clear day. Reproduction of painting used for the cover does not show the train which was in the extreme top left corner.

**61 — Henry Darrow**

Riding in a rented buggy on the road which connected Caribou with Eldora.

**62 — Mr. Baker's Mining Claim Cabin**

See #38.

**63 — Caribou Flats**

**64 — Jersey Mill**

The old Jersey Mill Stamp and Ore Roaster were transported by oxen in the 1860's and set up at the south edge of Caribou. Mother and her brothers and sisters played on the old foundation just as we did years later.

**65 — Roy Hinman**

Riding his horse and driving cattle from the town.

**66 — George Coffin**

Shown using a wheelbarrow to carry rock and ore from the tunnel where he was seeking silver and gold. He did find a fair showing of silver there.

**67 — Hinman's Second Barn**

Dale Hinman unbuckling harness on his horses preparing to feed and water them. After both he and his horses had eaten and rested, they would make the return trip with loads of ore destined for either New Cardinal, which was the terminal for the Caribou Railway branch, or to Boulder.

**68 — Tony Harbol House**

He was the owner of the St. Louis Gold Mine and Mill.

**69 — Robertson House**

Uncle Frank Robertson and family lived here while he worked as the hoist engineer on the Tillman Silver and Gold Mine for a year or so. His family consisted of Aunt Tillie and our cousins Sammie, May and Janie.

**70 — Henry Darrow House**

He married our 1903 school teacher, Miss Marshall, who later left him. He was fatally injured in an accident (I believe it was a horse and buggy runaway) about 1914 in the vicinity of the Apex Mine near Eldora. This Apex Mine, and two other patents, were leased by myself and my brothers when we prospected in our spare time during the 1920's and 1930's. See "Prospecting in the 1920's."

**71 — Coffin Home**

George and Lewis Coffin resided here as did their sister, Edna. After the fire of the winter of 1905-06, Cap Trollope moved his salvaged possessions into the Coffin House and remained there until they moved to Nederland about 1912. They operated a boarding house at Nederland during the Tungsten Boom which ended in 1918. Then they located in Boulder in the vicinity of 18th and Pearl streets. They died sometime in the 1920's.

**72 — Foundation of Old House**

One of our favorite places to stay. We concocted mud pies and it was here that cousin May Robertson made a mud pie and gave me a taste of it. I still feel as though I should spit when I think of that terrible moment.

**73 — Abandoned Silver Mine**

We children had the dangerous, but fun, pastime of leaning far out over the top of the shaft, tossing a rock down and listening to the splash as it hit the water far below.

**74 — Horse and Buggy**

**75, 76, and 77 — Carrying Water**

Water was sometimes carried in pails fastened to yokes over the shoulders.

**78 — Burro Outside Barn**

There were many burros around Caribou at that time.

**79 — Miners**

Going on shift at the St. Louis Mine from their lodging at the Trollope Hotel.

**80 — Caribou Park**

Now a peat bog.

**81 — Watering Trough for Horses**

Hewed out of a huge spruce log by John Hiney and placed at the main water supply. See #27 and #40.

**82 — Old Mine Hole**

Another one of our playgrounds as children where we entertained ourselves by throwing rocks. This hole was located on the west side of Goat Rock Mountain.

**83 — Cap Trollope**

Cap Trollope splitting wood at the rear yard of the hotel.

**84 — Caribou Cemetery**

Caribou's Cemetery is 300 feet north of #84.

**85 — First Water Reservoir**

Was Caribou's first water reservoir when it had fire hydrants in the 1870's.

# CARIBOU

# 3

There was only one reason for the founding of Nederland: the discovery of silver at Caribou.

It was the Caribou Mine, discovered 10 years before the great Leadville strikes, that put Colorado on the mining map and gave it the name "Silver State." At one time, the Caribou was acclaimed the richest silver mine in the world.

East of the mine, in a secluded mountain valley only four miles from the Continental Divide, a boom camp grew into the vigorous, proud and thriving town, Caribou. The town lasted for only 35 years. Today it is a ghost.

A variety of conditions worked against survival. In its high and isolated setting, Caribou was always at the mercy of the elements — furious winds and rainstorms, winter blizzards with snowdrifts of incredible depths, and three disastrous fires. Numerous homes and mine buildings were lost in 1877 in the first fire. The Caribou Mine building with all its valuable machinery was destroyed. Fires of 1899 and 1905 leveled large portions of the town. Scarlet fever and diphtheria epidemics took the lives of many.

Decreasing prices of silver, increasing costs of mining, continuing problems with the great flow of underground water and finally, the collapse of the silver market in 1893 — all had their depressing effects. Economic conditions forced many miners to abandon Caribou in search of work elsewhere.

The appealing story of this ghost town has inspired numerous writers and remains a permanent part of Nederland's past. Caribou gave Nederland its start in life.

Caribou in 1873 — William Henry Jackson's photograph of Caribou with Arapaho Peak and Baldy in the background. Caribou Hill is in the upper left.

Today, the townsite of Caribou is a quiet landscape with few marks of civilization. Two rather large stone ruins may be identified as remnants of the two oldest establishments in town. The first was originally the Leo Donnelly General Store, rebuilt in 1928 as a rooming and boarding house by the Potosi Mining Company. The other started out as Sears & Werley Billiard Hall, the largest building in Caribou. Originally a two-story building, it, too, was probably used by the Potosi Company. See numbers 43 and 44 in descriptions of William S. Smith's painting of Caribou.

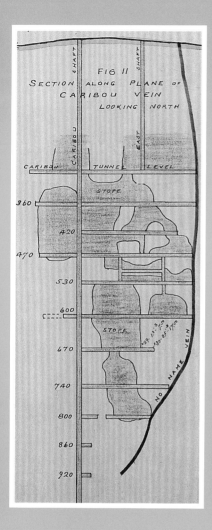

FIG. 11

SECTION ALONG PLANE OF
CARIBOU VEIN
LOOKING NORTH

The Caribou Mine was a producing mine by 1870, earning handsome profits. The main shaft was 740 feet deep by 1879, and by 1882 it had passed the 1000-foot level. These cutaway diagrams show the numerous shafts and levels and give some idea of the mine's tremendous size. During the first 10 years, the great mine justified the highest hopes of its various owners.

On January 1, 1883, the Caribou Mine closed for the first time, and from this date it started to decline. Accumulated problems, not lack of ore, caused the closing. The mine had been developed and exploited, experiencing periods of good and bad management, never being owned and operated by any one mining company. Between 1883 and 1900, several attempts to open the mine to full-scale production were made, but none were ever successful.

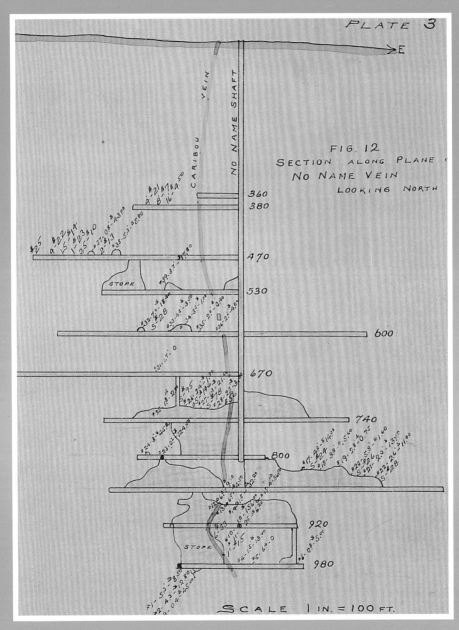

Caribou Mine

30

Caribou Mine

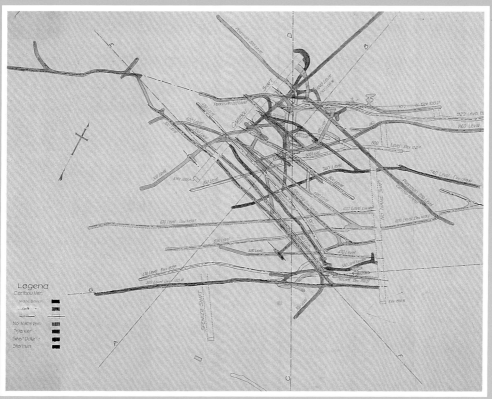

The New Jersey Mill — Built in 1876, it was not a successful venture, due to a variety of misfortunes. The rock foundation at the extreme right is all that is left on the site today.

Rock foundation remains at the site of the New Jersey Mill, 1987.

Caribou Cemetery, Summer 1988

This cabin is the only structure standing today in the Caribou townsite, and it may have been built after 1967. See description number 3 in William S. Smith's painting of Caribou.

Pike and Billy Bryant — An old photograph, remarkable because it is made with so little light and yet shows so clearly these two men in a tunnel underground. John Jackson of Tungsten comments: "They are hand drilling; they're using the double-jack method. Their light is a candle held in place by an iron candle holder they have stuck in the rock wall. Their steels are leaning against the wall under the candle."

The Strike

Tom Hendricks emerging from a lower level of the Cross Mine

Tom Hendricks reopened the Cross Mine in 1973, just a century after its discovery on July 11, 1873. Today, blasts of dynamite shake the mountain below the old townsite of Caribou. Tom is shown in the picture on page 38 climbing a ladder into the hoist room, located 160 feet directly beneath old Caribou. From the hoist room, a tunnel leads to the mine entrance. The ladder Tom is climbing leads to four lower levels and reaches 200 feet deeper into the earth.

Mining methods have changed since the time of Pike and Billy Bryant, shown on page 36. Pneumatic rock drills make the present day method much faster. But despite modern technology, mining is obviously hard work. Only a short tour of Tom Hendricks' mine is enough to convince anyone of this fact.

According to the Colorado Mining Association, there are only about five continuously operating small gold mines left in Colorado. The Hendricks Mine is one.

During 16 years of successful mine management work, Tom Hendricks and the Hendricks Mining Company have been the focus of a wide variety of featured stories in magazines, newspapers, and programs on radio and TV stations. One of the most interesting was produced by Mark Clayton for the **Christian Science Monitor** on November 1, 1988. Clayton wrote:

> Like the adventuring gold miners of American history, Mr. Hendricks' story has its own, modern-day romance. In the tradition of striking out with a few coins and a dream, he used a Master Card to charge a plane ticket to California 15 years ago — where, at age 23, he persuaded the owners of the Cross Mine to let him lease the old facility. Starting with just a pick and shovel, Hendricks reopened the mine by himself in 1973.

"Welcome to Caribou (population 2)." This catchy sentence was the first in Mark Clayton's fine article. Perhaps Caribou isn't exactly a ghost town after all.

# ELDORA

## 4

Gold discoveries in Eldora gave Nederland's economy a much needed boost in the 1890s. Most of the town's population disappeared when the silver boom ended, but the Bryant, Hetzer and McKenzie families, all prominent during the silver era, remained. The excitement of gold brought renewed optimism and new business to the area.

John Kemp, a prospector from Central City, was one of the first to discover gold at Eldora, locating Happy Valley Placer in 1891. Kemp worked the placer with seven partners. Within a year, other prospectors were rushing into the area, and soon mining claims of great promise were being made. Promoters greatly exaggerated the value of gold discoveries, helping to create a boom, one of the last of the old wild-day stampedes.

Gradually, business in nearby Nederland improved. By 1896, the old Caribou Mill, converted to refine gold, was running again. Nederland welcomed these changes, and newcomers restored the population.

More than one-half of the claims around Eldora were located on Spencer Mountain. These discoveries led to the development of the Mogul Tunnel. Cut at a depth of 600 to 1,000 feet below the surface veins of prominent properties, driven 2,600 feet into Spencer Mountain, the huge Mogul Tunnel was intended as a drainage and transportation enterprise. Hopes were high that an era of deep mining would result and prove highly profitable. Backers of the tunnel believed it had a production potential of hundreds of tons a day, but it never produced one-tenth of that amount.

Colonel Samuel B. Dick, a Civil War veteran, was one of the investors in the Mogul Tunnel. His business interests included other Boulder County mining properties as well as the Colorado & Northern Railroad, the Switzerland Trail of America. Colonel Dick was one of the group of wealthy Eastern men who built the C&N to Ward — men who had made their money in railroads, lumber and steel.

From 1900 on, Colonel Dick wanted to build the C&N to Eldora, and he visualized building on over the Continental Divide into Middle Park. When the Moffat Railroad was built over Rollins Pass, he thought the Eldora extension should connect with it. Many mines lacked the convenience of railroad service; providing it was Colonel Dick's ambition. Especially, he wanted to serve the Mogul Tunnel which he thought was a "sure thing."

By 1901, Colonel Dick owned controlling interest in the

Switzerland Trail, and three years later became president of the road. Then he built the Eldora line, completely dedicated to the future of mining and to the future of his railroad. The first train to Eldora arrived on December 19, 1904, before the railroad track was completely finished. Rails ended that day more than a mile from town. Those aboard — officials, bankers and crew — cheerfully hiked the remaining distance. Jubilant citizens met the travelers and escorted them to the still-standing Gold Miner Hotel for a turkey dinner in celebration of the event. Regular railroad service started early in January 1905.

Eldora's gold boom had a short history. Basically, the gold boom was over by 1900. Long before the railroad arrived, mining had dwindled to only a fraction of its former activity. The disheartening fact was: Gold mining in Eldora was simply not profitable. Surface veins yielded high profits, but as greater depths were reached, nearly all the mines contained low grade ore that could not be milled profitably.

Eldora's gold boom stimulated Nederland, nevertheless, and by the time it was over, tungsten mining had begun. Within a few years, the Wolf Tongue Mining Company was organized. The old Caribou Mill was remodeled again, this time for processing tungsten.

Gold from Eldora can be found in a world famous collection of minerals owned by Queen Victoria of England.

The fine specimen given to Her Majesty contains free gold. It was taken from the Virginia Mine on Spencer Mountain.

Eldora Ski Area goes back in history to 1962 and the Ertl family who operated it successfully for many years. The resort declined in the early 1980s and was closed completely during the season of 1986-87. Business establishments in Nederland as well as those in nearby areas suffered greatly that season. Some were unable to survive at all with the resort closed. Winter economy in the Nederland area depends on Eldora to bring skiers to their restaurants, shops and places to stay overnight.

In early September 1987, the Ertls made an announcement: Eldora would open in November for the ski season of 1987-88 under the management of Andy Daly, a man with an impressive background and experience. Daly acquired the resort through a lease-purchase agreement with the Ertls, shocking Colorado's ski industry when he resigned (after eight years as president of Copper Mountain) to open Eldora. The Ertls' announcement was exhilarating news for the town of Nederland, although at first some residents hesitated to think Eldora could be run by anyone but the Ertls.

Daly promised "good service and top flight operation both on and off the hill." He enlisted the expert assistance of Dean Cox, former president and general manager of Silver Creek, who accepted the position of general manager.

The Alpenhorn Lodge was completely remodeled, given fresh paint and new carpeting. Numerous attractive programs, reasonably priced, were offered. Skiers responded. More than 100,000 guests contributed to a successful first season under the new management.

In the 1988-89 season, Eldora's management announced Jim Isham as skier services manager. In his eight years at Copper Mountain, Isham's ski school became a nationally recognized leader in ski instruction and he promised to provide the same top notch service at Eldora.

Beginners at Eldora in 1988-89 enjoyed a new surface lift called Tenderfoot. Also new was Porcupine Park, a cross-country trail "gently rolling through pine forests, perfect for a family outing."

Perhaps the most exciting change, which very nearly doubled the size of Eldora's ski area, was the reopening of Corona Bowl. Corona opened in January 1989, for the first time in eight years. On the backside of Eldora Mountain, Corona offers challenging skiing for experts and intermediates.

Corona takes its name from the station at the top of Rollins Pass where the old railroad route crossed the Continental Divide before the Moffat Tunnel was built. From the warming shelter at the top of Corona, there are spectacular views of Rollins Pass, the Arapaho Peaks, James Peak and the northern part of the Continental Divide.

Eldora is one of Colorado's leading snowboard centers, with perfect terrain for learning. Cross-country skiing is extensive. Judy Gallian, who lives in the vicinity of Golden Gate Canyon, said Eldora cross-country trails are "great skiing — you can really get out by yourself. Downhillers get a kick out of seeing skinny skis on the slopes." Night skiing on 15 lighted trails is a major part of Eldora's operation. Eldora offers special programs for children, special days for women and days for those who have never skied before. RTD bus service directly to Eldora takes only 45 minutes from Boulder.

Skiing at Eldora is fun, say those who have tried it. "The resort is small, but it's more friendly. Prices are reasonable, and it's great for family skiing," said Kay Zueck of Denver.

Eldora's management team said their goal is "to bring Eldora to its full potential" and give quality, convenience, reasonable prices and great choices.

Some of this information on skiing at Eldora was furnished through the courtesy of Tom Mills, marketing director, Eldora Mountain Resort.

John Kemp's cabin was one of the first built in Eldora. Kemp's wife, his two sons and Moses the burro are shown in foreground. Donald C. Kemp, author of **Silver, Gold and Black Iron,** is one of the young sons pictured here.

On the road to Eldora 1897

Eldora Stage 1898

Windlass for hoisting ore

Pulley, frame & Windlass
housing - near Eldora.

Gold Miner Hotel in Eldora looks essentially the same as it looked in 1897, the year it was built. A sturdy log survivor of gold boom days, it is now a bed and breakfast establishment advertising "mountain-sized breakfasts" and the nearest location to Eldora skiing where there is "great cross-country skiing."

Continental Divide region near Nederland

Eldora Ski Lift, Early 1988

Alpenhorn Lodge is a day lodge with full-service rental facilities and a child care center.

# TUNGSTEN MINING

## 5

In the year 1900, a rare Colorado metal was waiting to be discovered, waiting to make Nederland world famous. Kicked aside by gold and silver seekers as a worthless nuisance and contemptuously called "that damned black iron," tungsten lay in plain sight on mountain slopes around Nederland, unrecognized for what it was — a semiprecious metal. But the tungsten boom was brewing, and the 20th century would bring dramatic change.

Nederland was on the western edge of a small area, about four miles wide and nine miles long, called the tungsten district. The area was unusual, lacking gold and silver, but having millions of dollars worth of rare tungsten. Even the ore was unusual; it lacked the troublesome materials commonly associated with tungsten ores found in other parts of the world.

**Mining in Boulder County** reported the following:

Until the year 1900 when it first became known that the ore commonly called "black iron" was a valuable rare metal, the territory now known as the tungsten district was considered barren and worthless though surrounded on all sides by gold and silver bearing veins. Samuel P. Conger, the veteran prospector who twenty years before had discovered the old Caribou silver mine, near what is now the western borders of the tungsten field, learned the true character of the ore from a partner who had mined wolframite ore in Arizona; and secured a lease on a tract of land on the Boulder County Ranch, opened up the Conger lead, which later proved to be the greatest tungsten mine ever discovered, its output being valued well above $1,000,000.

Veteran prospector Sam Conger described events leading up to the sale of his lease to Robert M. Bell of Canada. First, Conger gathered samples of ore and brought them to Denver from the location he remembered on Boulder County Ranch. Conger and his partner, Nelson Wannamaker, then took the samples to various establishments to have them assayed. Out of five opinions, two assayers said the samples were tungsten. Immediately, the two men secured a lease and began to work the property. Conger told Thomas Dawson of the Colorado Historical Society:

It was no time until we had arranged with a European house to ship the ore across the water. We sent a great deal of it away and made a sufficient success of the enterprise to sell our lease for $5000, Dr. Bell, of Canada, being the purchaser.

Robert M. Bell was the first developer of the Conger Mine. Chauncey F. Lake, who was managing the Boulder County

Mine at Cardinal, took over management of the undeveloped mine. Dawson recorded Conger's statement:

Professor Lake named the mine for me, and it is still known as the Conger.

In its day the Conger Mine was known as the greatest tungsten mine in the world. Today the only remaining building at the site is a wooden loadout chute at the bottom of the old waste dump. At the top of the dump, one of the main shafts is permanently blocked by an eight-inch-thick concrete slab which safeguards the abandoned mine. The Conger could be reopened in the future if market conditions made tungsten mining profitable again in Colorado. The huge waste dump on Illinois Hill is slowly disappearing as the refuse rock is hauled away and used for roadbed to make highway improvements.

Before 1900, steel manufacturers used tungsten secretly, because production was so small and the world supply so limited. For many years they had known that a certain percentage of tungsten alloyed with steel produced a metal that could hold its temper under a high degree of heat, a metal particularly adapted to the making of high-speed tool steel. Discoveries in Australia soon followed those made in Nederland, creating a dependable supply. The new abundant supply resulted in a steady and constant demand by manufacturers.

Nederland's boom began as soon as tungsten was known

to be rare and valuable. The first two companies organized to mine, mill and purchase tungsten were Chauncey Lake's Company (The Conger Mine and others) and the Great Western Exploration and Reduction Company. All the tungsten ore produced by these two companies was purchased by the Primos Chemical Company of Primos, Pennsylvania, the world's largest dealer in tungsten ore and its products.

A third company was organized in 1904, The Wolf Tongue Mining and Milling Company. The name "Wolf Tongue" is a combination of two words. Many people called tungsten ore "wolfram" and others called it "tungsten." By changing the spelling slightly, the company came up with an imaginative name.

The Wolf Tongue Company was a subsidiary of Firth Sterling Steel of McKeesport, Pennsylvania. Firth Sterling had a large projectile factory in Washington, D.C., in addition to its steel mills at McKeesport. The Wolf Tongue Company bought many mines around Nederland including the Oregon, the Clyde, the Illinois and the Cold Spring, which was the richest.

For processing ores, they bought the old Caribou Mill in Nederland which had lain intermittently idle since 1885. New and modern machines were installed. All the tungsten from mines of the Wolf Tongue Company was processed at the old historic mill, shipped to McKeesport and used in the steel mills of Firth Sterling.

During the early years of the 1900s, steel manufacturers Stein and Boericke became increasingly interested in the Conger Mine. First, they acquired control of the Primos Chemical Company; then in 1905 they merged with Great Western Exploration of Colorado under a new name: Stein and Boericke Mining and Milling Company. Three years later, by consolidating with the extensive holdings of Boulder County Ranch, Stein and Boericke acquired the Conger Mine. Chauncey Lake, who had managed the Conger Mine from the first, became resident manager of this huge new company, the Primos Mining and Milling Company. The Primos Company built the largest tungsten mill in the world not far from the Conger Mine. A small company town called Lakewood grew up near the mill.

With the availability of tungsten to the steel industry, dynamic changes took place in American industry. Automobile manufacturers found that cylinders, piston rings, valves and other working parts subject to the fierce heat of burning gasoline were far superior if made of tungsten steel. Tungsten in its various forms (such as calcium tungstate, tungstate salts and lead tungstate) and in its various alloys became useful in many ways: in making x-rays visible, in coloring glass, in glazing porcelain, in making filaments for electric lamps and wire for dental work. Many other uses were partially worked out, others were suggested, but the most extensive use was in tool manufacturing.

Nederland prospered. Million-dollar tungsten mines meant big business for a growing town. But three other significant events further changed Nederland. First was the C&N Railroad which came to town in 1904. Next was the building of Barker Dam during the years 1907-1910. The third big change, the automobile, revolutionized transportation.

In the mining industry, the first 10 years of the 20th century ended with a year of record production for both the Wolf Tongue and Primos companies. During the next four years, 1910-1914, foreign competition was keenly felt. Nederland no longer had a monopoly on production of tungsten. Burma, Australia and New Zealand contributed greatly to the world market, bringing American tungsten prices down to their lowest point. Thus, at the outbreak of the European war in 1914, the American market was depressingly quiet — a lull before the storm. When Great Britain placed an embargo on shipment of tungsten ore from its empire, American tungsten was suddenly in great demand. Prices rose dramatically. Called the "key mineral" of the war, tungsten was vitally needed in the production of war materials. Nederland responded, producing thousands of tons of the metal.

By 1915, the Wolf Tongue Company and the Primos

Company were running their facilities at full capacity, operating 24 hours a day, seven days a week. Also contributing to production were three other newly organized companies. Nederland's greatest fame and prosperity came with the peak of the tungsten boom in 1916. Production in that one year alone exceeded $4 million.

Brought on by the First World War, a big rush to the tungsten fields started in the spring of 1915. The tremendous influx of tungsten hunters streaming into Nederland was one of the last stampedes in Colorado mining history. Three motor stage lines brought fortune hunters up the canyon by the hundreds. Only a year before, there was hardly enough business to keep stage lines in operation. Nederland's tungsten boom was heading for an impressive climax during the war years, 1914-1917.

Nederland was transformed. Nine new residential sections were added in just one year; only one had been added in all the previous years of the tungsten boom. Houses sprung up like mushrooms, and the little village of 300 souls suddenly became a town of 3,000 or more inhabitants by 1916. Surrounding areas were estimated to have an additional 2,000 persons, both men and women, who were combing every foot of the region in their frenzied rush for wealth.

There were five hotels in town, several rooming and boarding houses, all filled to overflowing with temporary residents. As crowds grew steadily greater, beds had to be rented in eight-hour shifts, and customers in various eating places were allowed only 20 minutes to eat a meal.

Outside town in every possible place, tents and shacks housed additional hundreds who hoped to strike it rich. M.B. Tomblin, then secretary of the State Bureau of Mines, described this period as follows:

There never has been a mining discovery in Colorado where the small operator has received so much benefit as in the tungsten fields. There are dozens who have cleaned up fortunes in the last year.

By 1917 the great boom began to collapse. When the action ceased, mineral hunters departed as fast as they had come. Houses, cabins, shacks — many were simply left standing vacant and deserted. Mining continued after the boom, although at a much slower pace. Tungsten imported from China in 1919 and shipped to the United States as ballast on freighters caused further decline. Finally, in 1921 the mining business stopped altogether. The huge Primos Company disappeared altogether. The Vanadium Corporation of America bought the entire property and soon afterwards sold everything but the land to L.D. Wells, a mine-equipment dealer in Boulder. Wells dismantled and removed the town of Lakewood and the Primos Mill with all its machinery.

The Wolf Tongue Company, in contrast, was back in business again by the end of 1922. Production from company-owned mines, along with production of small independent operators, kept the mill steadily operating for many years. A fire in 1926 destroyed the old mill, but the Wolf Tongue Company immediately built a new fireproof mill on the same site. During the Second World War and again during the Korean War, tungsten was needed for the war effort. Shafts and tunnels of many Nederland area mines were unwatered, retimbered and put back into working order.

The mammoth Conger Mine, property of the Vanadium Corporation of America, was reopened in 1938 and operated steadily for six and one-half years. When it closed, equipment was completely removed from the Conger. Robert Sterling, supervisor of Conger operations, said that a shortage of competent mine and mill labor was the reason for closing. The company had hoped to do more development work when the labor shortage hit.

Tungsten ore sample

Load out chute at the bottom of Conger waste dump

Shaft closure, Conger Mine

Conger Mine

In its day, the Primos Mill was the largest tungsten mill in the world. Chauncey F. Lake, resident manager, lived in the house (left foreground).

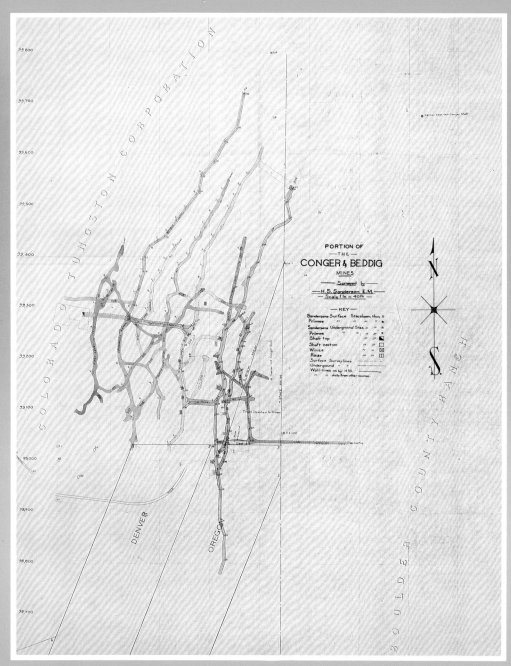

Conger Mine, bird's-eye view

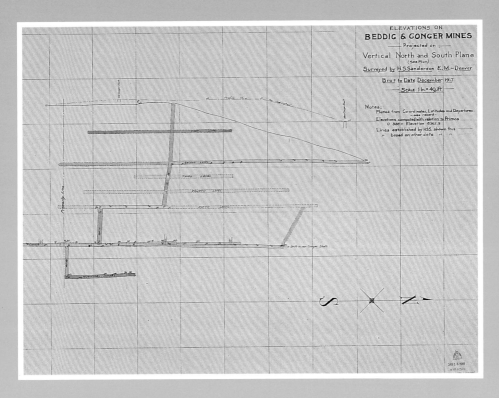

Sectional drawing of Conger Mine

The Hetzer House opened its doors for business July 4, 1877. **Boulder County News** of July 20, 1877, recommended the new hotel to travelers, declaring it "second to none in the hill country." Hetzer House was famous throughout Boulder County for more than 60 years. It suffered the fate of many early buildings in Nederland, being completely destroyed by a fire in December 1939.

The Antlers Hotel, named after a famous hotel in Colorado Springs, was finished in 1897. Mary Roose, a Boulder woman with six children, moved to Nederland after her husband's death. Mrs. Roose had the hotel built as a home and business combined. Family living quarters, kitchens, dining room and office occupied the first floor, and there were 14 guest bedrooms on the second floor. Mrs. Roose operated her hotel for summer tourist business, but during the years of the tungsten boom, it was open all year.

During the flu epidemic of 1917, the Antlers was converted to a hospital. Many people of Nederland donated money to equip the hospital. Robert Sterling of the Vanadium Corporation, Louis Firth of the Wolf Tongue Company, and officials of other large companies gave money, hired nurses and personally helped in many ways.

This building, like the Hetzer House, survived for more than 60 years. The Antlers was torn down in 1961 to allow for expansion of St. Rita's Catholic Church.

Old Pike Stroud's flopping joint — colorful housing in boom town Nederland

Irene Smith graciously gave her permission to photograph the retaining wall along her driveway which contains artifacts from the Conger Mine. Irene's husband, Joe, was manager of the Conger Mine at one time. He assembled the artifacts so skillfully, the finished job is like a work of art.

# SAM CONGER

## 6

Sam Conger was born in Monroe County, Ohio, on July 1, 1833, and left home at age 17 to make his way in the world. Crossing the Great Plains in a wagon bearing on its canvas the famous slogan "Pike's Peak or Bust," he arrived in Colorado in 1860.

Known facts about Conger's life seem to be few. He prospected for lead in Wisconsin, worked for short periods in California and Oregon, but spent most of his life in Colorado. At first, he worked around Central City — exploring, hunting, prospecting. Although Indians and mountain men of earlier eras must have explored Nederland Valley, the only record of a hunter there is that of Sam Conger in 1864. "I've prospected almost every foot of the mountains in northern Colorado. After covering them afoot almost continuously for 60 years, I ought to know them, oughtn't I?" he told author Forbes Parkhill in an interview of 1921.

Sam Conger discovered the famous Caribou silver mine in

1868. The first published report of this event is found in the **Rocky Mountain Directory and Colorado Gazetteer** for 1871:

Mr. Conger was the first white man who explored this wild mountain region, and from his adventurous explorations the richest silver mining district in Colorado or the world, has been discovered and developed. This discovery was recorded as the Caribou lode, now the great silver mine of Colorado.

Very much aware that another man claimed to have discovered the Caribou Mine, Conger told Thomas Dawson in an unpublished interview for the Colorado Historical Society:

I know that Bill Martin claims to have made the discovery. I don't know whether he is a little looney or just mean. I once thought of putting him through for his stories, but since have thought better of it and have concluded to let him talk. He is an old man now, living in Boulder, and he can't do much more harm.

Although claims of the two men are controversial, they do not diminish the importance of the Caribou Mine or its importance in Nederland's early history. Almost all Colorado historians have given Sam Conger the credit he always claimed.

More than 30 years later, Conger discovered tungsten at Nederland. The developed mine became known as the Conger. The Dawson Scrapbook in the Colorado Historical Society contains the following:

The credit for the discovery of tungsten ore in Boulder County is rightly given to Samuel P. Conger, a veteran prospector . . . He discovered more veins in Boulder County than any other man, and most of them have turned out rich mines. But if he had found nothing else of value, the discovery of tungsten would alone have made him famous.

Sam Conger's two major discoveries, silver and tungsten, relate directly to Nederland's development and historical importance, and his name as a Nederland pioneer is significant. "Conger, grand old man of the mountains, has made and lost three fortunes," wrote author Forbes Parkhill in **The Denver Post** of December 18, 1921.

Conger can claim credit as a scout in the Indian wars, but he doesn't. Friends say he was a government scout during the Indian wars, and was a close friend of "Buffalo Bill" Cody. He is entitled to draw a pension for these services, friends say, but is too proud to apply for the pension, feeling that he is capable of making his own way in the world, and that no man should ask for a pension from the government merely because of advanced age.

Veteran prospector Sam Conger reached his last years of life without the comfortable feeling of financial security despite having earned considerable sums of money. He died in Denver on October 23, 1925, after only a few days' illness. He lived 92 years, actively working in the Colorado mountains, prospecting to the end.

Pioneer prospector Sam Conger, 1833-1925

Genuine prospectors never mine. It is seldom that they dig a hole more than 25 feet deep, and very few have ever dug more than 10 feet. They find properties to sell. That is their business. They cannot content themselves with the daily humdrum life of the miner underground. A tent is their natural house, and a windlass is the only mining machinery they care to know anything about. Like the birds, they are never so happy as when on the wing to some new, untried and wild region.

(This description was written by W.C. Wynkoop, editor of **Mining Industry and Tradesman,** June 23, 1892.)

Primitive hand windlass

TOM BERGER WPA

Transportation in 1860s

The prospector's helper

# TRANSPORTATION

## 7

THE SWITZERLAND TRAIL OF AMERICA

This little narrow-gauge road started out in 1883 as the
Greeley, Salt Lake & Pacific Railroad. The name is
remarkable. Its trains never departed from Greeley, never
were closer to Salt Lake City than Sunset, and never
anywhere near the Pacific Ocean.

Greeley, Salt Lake & Pacific trains departed from
Boulder, went up Boulder Canyon as far as Orodell where
they turned into Four Mile Canyon and traveled west to
Sunset, 14 steep and scenic miles. Along the way, four stops
were made. The railroad was built primarily for hauling
supplies to the mines and hauling ore out, but tourism was
promoted from the first. The railroad built a dance pavilion
and provided picnic grounds at Sunset, the end of the line.
Organizations such as the Elks, the Grocers, and the
Methodists held annual picnics. Wildflower specials were
favorite train rides featuring stops at selected places so
passengers could gather mountain flowers.

For the first five years, there was no turntable or wye at Sunset; trains had to be backed down to Boulder. Amazingly, they operated without accident.

The Greeley, Salt Lake & Pacific Railroad came to a tragic end in 1894. A cloudburst sent a great flood down the canyons, wiping out bridges, wagon roads and almost every mile of railroad right-of-way.

Four years later, in 1898, the Colorado & Northwestern built a new line above flood level. Later that year, the line was extended from Sunset to Ward and hailed as the finest narrow-gauge road ever built in the United States. With the C&N railroad came a famous name, "The Switzerland Trail of America" — a name which remained through subsequent bankruptcies and reorganizations of the railroad until the end of its life.

Tourism was more widely promoted than ever before. On a mountainside between Sunset and Ward, the C&N built Mont Alto Park in a grove of giant Ponderosa pines. It was opened on July 15, 1898. Here they laid out extensive grounds with picnic tables, a baseball field and a huge rustic dance pavilion. A fountain fed by spring water (built of native rock, jagged white quartz and colorful blocks of red sandstone) was an inviting spot, a perfect place for taking pictures.

The railroad encouraged travel groups by offering special rates. They continued wildflower specials, ran autumn leaf excursions, and added a famous moonlight ride. The Boulder **Daily Camera** of July 25, 1898, described the new ride:

A midnight ride through beautiful Boulder Canyon, over picturesque Mont Alto and beyond is the plan of the C&N management . . . the moon will be full, the beauty and splendor of the canyon will be at its height and the trip will furnish a ride of such fascinating beauty that none can resist it.

When the Switzerland Trail was extended to Eldora, climbing a dangerous winding road beyond Sunset, another picnic area was developed at Glacier Lake. The C&N removed the pavilion at Mont Alto, taking it down in sections and transporting it to Glacier Lake on flatcars. There it was set up again, improved and enlarged in time for the tourist season of 1905.

Cardinal was the stop for Nederland, about two miles west of town. Advertising the new route "A Trip to Cloudland" in a railroad folder, the C&N promised a journey new and novel, one a traveler would want to repeat. "When you come to Colorado you cannot do better than indulge in a trip to Cloudland," began the advertising which elaborated:

The finely appointed trains of the Colorado and Northwestern leave the Denver Union Depot and without any change of cars convey the traveler to the crest of the continent in a little less than three hours, traversing a distance of fifty miles and unfolding a volume of panoramic beauty unequaled in the world. In this time one is transported from the noise and heat of the city to the snow-clad peaks that are constantly in view as the train gently ascends to the sky-line without traversing a single tunnel or encountering any other discomforts of mountain travel.

From the beginning, various owners of this narrow-gauge line had spent large sums of money promoting business and trying to operate the road without loss. Excursion trains were good business, but the year-round hauling of supplies to the mines and hauling ore out was the road's vital need for a healthy profit.

Railroad revenues were greatest when Barker Dam was being constructed. Trains hauling supplies and equipment to the dam site went through Cardinal to Sulphide, a little settlement between Cardinal and Eldora. There a temporary line, owned and operated by the construction company, went east about four miles to the dam site.

Days of building Barker Dam were exciting, happy days; the Switzerland Trail had its own special work to do for the big project. The railroad had two new freight locomotives, one a Shay, a noisy contraption affectionately referred to as a "coffee grinder." It was a powerful geared engine having a maximum speed of about 12 miles per hour, but it could pull a tremendous load and hauled much of the machinery for the dam. Elbert Hubbard, who later worked as a brakeman and fireman on the road, said:

I remember when they took up the big railroad type steam shovel. The 25 (Shay) was pulling it . . . That's all it had, except the caboose. The 25 was slow and it was going extra slow that day. That steam shovel was very heavy, and I think they were afraid of the rails spreading.

Oscar Bernsten was a fireman on the C&N and he remembered:

When they were building Nederland Dam, we used to go out of here at 6 o'clock in the morning with 12 cars of cement and the caboose. Twenty tons in each car, and brother, we sure had to scratch between here and Sunset to make it.

The grade between Boulder and Sunset was one of the steepest that narrow-gauge trains had to travel in reaching their destination at Sulphide. It was a climb of nearly 1,000 feet.

The dam under construction was a lively sight. Groups on holiday (the Baptist Young People's Union, the Danish Societies, and the United Brotherhood of Leather Workers, for example) rode the train to Barker Dam for a firsthand look at the work in progress.

The Switzerland Trail of America came to an end in 1919. Railroad revenues gradually decreased after 1911, owing to the rapid development of the automobile and a steady decline in mining. Thus when another cloudburst, as devastating as the one in 1894, flooded canyons and caused extensive damage, it hastened the inevitable. The system and all its equipment were sold; even rails were taken up. One locomotive was sent to Alaska. Other equipment went to the Saratoga-Encampment road in Wyoming. Some was sent to California, some to Louisiana, and 5,000 tons of equipment were shipped to Kobe, Japan.

In a day when serious wrecks happened all over the country on other railroad lines, the Switzerland Trail of America had very nearly a perfect record — astonishing in a route with such heavy grades, so many rock cuts and sharp curves, and so many trestles. Railroadmen considered this more than an achievement; it was the next thing to a miracle.

By inventing and manufacturing the Stanley Steamer, Freelan Stanley and his twin brother Francis Stanley made permanent changes in the transportation life of Boulder Canyon and Nederland.

One summer day in 1910, the first horseless carriage ever driven up the one-way road came steaming into Nederland on its own power. Robert Heintz, operating a Stanley Steamer, successfully negotiated the challenging wagon road — quite a feat for both machine and driver. Stanley Steamers were notoriously hard to operate, depending on an open fire and hot steam for power, and the Boulder Canyon wagon road was no easy road to drive with its dust, sharp curves and steep grades. Townspeople joyfully hailed the new invention and its trial run, which suggested prospects of an auto stage line for Nederland.

It was well-known that travelers to Estes Park were making the trip in Stanley Steamers. Freelan Stanley came to Colorado for his health, fell in love with Estes Park and built the Stanley Hotel. He provided transportation by "steamer" for his guests. Although Estes Park was one of the first places to enjoy the automobile, within a year there was daily round-trip service between Boulder and Nederland.

Canyon traffic became a serious problem. Teamsters cursed the new contraption that frightened horses and was difficult to pass on the narrow wagon road.

The new horseless carriage, nevertheless, had come to stay; the old wagon road had to change. Convicts from the state penitentiary at Canon City rebuilt the old 1871 Boulder Canyon Wagon Road during the years 1914 to 1919.

Robert Heintz' history-making drive up Boulder Canyon that summer day in 1910 marked the beginning of the end for all the colorful horse-powered vehicles — the various stagecoaches, the ore wagons, the many freight wagons with fascinating and varied cargo.

Freight wagons were operated by men called "freighters" or "teamsters." Generally they had four-horse outfits, but some had six. Some were mule outfits, some were made up of both horses and mules. Their cargo consisted of items such as horse feed, mine timbers, boilers for mills and machinery of all kinds. Each teamster had a dog running ahead to announce his owner's approach as well as numerous bells on his horse harness which rang merrily as the animals moved.

Roads were so steep and loads so heavy that in some places wheels had to be chained together for the downgrade so that instead of turning, the wheels would slide. This procedure was called roughlocking and kept wagons from running up on the wheel horses. Brake locks were used so constantly, they had to be renewed every few days.

These outfits with their long rows of red, white and blue harness rings, their tinkling bells, their various plumes and dyed horse-hair decorations were an inspiring sight. Young boys in particular found them fascinating and were always on the alert to pick up any new word from a teamster's vocabulary.

The Stanley brothers continued their production of steam automobiles until the early 1920s, although most pioneer car manufacturers in the United States had turned to gasoline power by 1910. At the end of the First World War, Ford dominated the scene, but within the next 10 years, two other giants — General Motors and the Chrysler Corporation — were leading producers of cars in the United States. Along with Ford, they became known as the "Big Three" in the automotive industry.

The success of the gasoline-powered automobile, its immediate public acceptance and popularity proved a severe blow to tourism on the Switzerland Trail railroad. The rapid rise of the automobile was one of the reasons given for abandonment of the line in 1919.

Jack Snyder lives in Nederland and vividly remembers the Kite and Glacier tourist service which featured seven-passenger touring cars. Arapaho Glacier was one of the big attractions for tourists of the day. From Denver, sightseers made the trip in three stages. First they came to Boulder via interurban railway known as the "Kite Route." From Boulder they rode in "Kite and Glacier" taxis to Nederland; and from Nederland to the glacier, they rode in more primitive style, on the backs of donkeys or horses.

"The taxis were seven-passenger canvas top touring cars," said Jack Snyder. "Glen Sherman drove the Cadillac, Jack Gilman drove the Lincoln, Seth Armstead drove the Packard."

Lover's Leap, Alps Lodge, Sugar Loaf Road, Red Sign Mine, an old tollhouse below Boulder Falls, the Eureka Mine and the Eccles Place were pointed out in Boulder Canyon in addition to places mentioned in the first chapter of this book. "At Ted Green's in Tungsten," Jack remembered, "there was a sign in summer which read 'WE HAVE POP ON ICE, BUT WE DON'T KNOW WHERE MOM IS.' "

Sunset Station — The railroad lines branched at Sunset, one going northwest to Ward, the other going southwest to Eldora.

Mont Alto Park shows the fountain in the foreground, dance pavilion in the background.

Cover of Railroad Folder

Shay Freight Engine

Freight Wagon in Boulder Canyon

Arapaho Glacier

Converted box car, once used on the Switzerland Trail

Round trip ticket to Eldora on the Switzerland Trail

Boulder Freight Depot

Narrow Gauge Steam Engine

# BARKER DAM

## 8

In the early 1900s, the State of Colorado needed electricity, and the mountains seemed to offer unlimited water resources. The Central Colorado Power Company planned several hydroelectric systems but built only two: one at Nederland and the Shoshone near Glenwood Springs.

Barker Dam and Reservoir were named for Mrs. Hannah Barker who owned the hay meadows where the dam was built. The Central Colorado Power Company (now Public Service), searching for a reservoir site, wanted to buy Mrs. Barker's land. She declined to sell. The power company then filed condemnation proceedings in the district court at Boulder. A jury decided the case in favor of the power company, and Mrs. Barker was awarded $23,000 for her ranch.

Boulder Hydro originates in Nederland with Barker Dam and Reservoir, the largest visible parts of a highly successful engineering feat. Water from Barker Reservoir begins its powermaking journey unseen and travels through a concrete gravity line, 11.7 miles directly east through the mountains, to Kossler Reservoir. From Kossler Reservoir it drops 1,828 feet through the penstock tube to run turbines which generate electricity at the power plant in lower Boulder Canyon.

The Colorado & Northwestern Railroad hauled large construction equipment to the dam site at Nederland. Included were two aerial tramways, a large sawmill and a railroad-type steam shovel. This particular type shovel was the same kind being used to dig the Panama Canal. Trains hauling supplies and equipment went through Cardinal and on to Sulphide over the famous narrow-gauge route called "The Switzerland Trail of America." From Sulphide, a temporary spur line, owned and operated by the construction company, went east to the dam site, about four miles.

Building the concrete gravity line from the reservoir at Nederland to Kossler Reservoir was reported to have been a more difficult construction job than the dam itself. **Town and Country Review** printed a newspaper in honor of Nederland's 100th birthday and reported that sections of the line were actually manufactured at various points along the route in order to avoid problems of transportation in the rugged mountain terrain.

The penstock tube carrying water from Kossler Reservoir to the power house was built of sections of steel pipe

52 inches in diameter in the upper sections, narrowing to 44-inch sections above the plant. At the bottom of its drop from Kossler Reservoir, water pressure measured 800 pounds per square inch where it entered the power house. At the time Boulder Hydro was built, this water pressure was higher than that of any other plant in the nation.

Work on Barker Dam was interrupted twice before the project was finished in 1910. The depression, known as the "Panic of 1907," caused work to cease until June 1908. The work of digging down to bedrock was finished in the fall of 1908, but again construction had to stop; concrete could not be poured in freezing weather. Work revived in the summer of 1909. On August 4, 1910, in a public ceremony at the power house, Alfred S. Greenman, mayor of Boulder, threw the lever that started giant 12,000-horsepower turbines.

Lawrence T. Paddock wrote this story in the Boulder **Daily Camera** of August 10, 1985:

On August 4, 1910, a big deal was made of the action of then Boulder Mayor Alfred A. Greenman flipping a switch to turn on the plant during the afternoon ceremony. According to PSCo Vice President Oscar Lee, the plant then was not quite ready to produce power. In the background at the ceremony was another man with another switch. He kept an eye on Mayor Greenman and closed the second switch at the moment the mayor closed the ceremonial one. The power that came on that day actually was from the Shoshone hydro plant.

The Boulder Hydroelectric System is considered one of

the greatest engineering feats in Boulder County. Little practical knowledge about such systems was available in the early 1900s, and the construction of Barker Dam provided answers to technical questions, information later used throughout the world. Today the power plant in Boulder Canyon is completely automated.

The first view of Nederland is always a surprise. For miles the drive up Boulder Canyon has been through pine forests and between rocky walls, following the stream the entire way. Below the town of Tungsten the canyon widens, and the road cuts through one or two small ranches before climbing the last hill to the breast of Barker Dam. Then suddenly as you reach the top, a striking panorama opens before you. At your feet lies the lake of the Barker Reservoir, stretching to the cluster of houses in the distance which is Nederland, while behind and beyond rise the snow-capped peaks of the Continental Divide. (Description by Muriel S. Wolle in **Stampede to Timberline**, page 495.)

William Henry Jackson's photograph, Nederland Park, was made during the 1873 Hayden Survey of Colorado. Jackson's team, buggy, and driver can be seen at the lower edge of the picture, waiting for him while he took the picture.

Drawing of a railroad-type steam shovel

The steam shovel used in construction of Barker Dam was hauled by a Shay freight engine over this road. Shown is a section of the roadbed between Sunset and Eldora. Photograph taken in summer 1988.

Barker Dam under construction

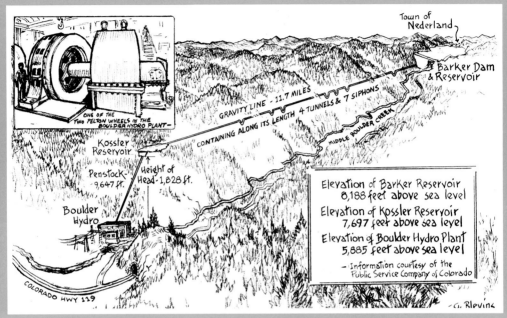

Town of Nederland

Barker Dam & Reservoir

GRAVITY LINE - 11.7 MILES
CONTAINING ALONG ITS LENGTH 4 TUNNELS & 7 SIPHONS

MIDDLE BOULDER CREEK

ONE OF THE TWO PELTON WHEELS IN THE BOULDER HYDRO PLANT—

Kossler Reservoir

Penstock- 9,647 ft.

Height of Head - 1,828 ft.

Boulder Hydro

COLORADO HWY 119

Elevation of Barker Reservoir
8,188 feet above sea level

Elevation of Kossler Reservoir
7,697 feet above sea level

Elevation of Boulder Hydro Plant
5,885 feet above sea level

— Information courtesy of the
Public Service Company of Colorado

-G. Blevins

After 18 months of construction, Barker Dam rose to its completed height of 175 feet and stretched across Boulder Creek, 720 feet at the crest.

Actually, construction of the gravity line to feed the hydro plant presented more engineering problems than the larger project of Barker Dam. Clearing of dense stands of timber, tunneling, and mountain-moving for necessary side-hill cuts were among the thorny puzzles to be solved.

Construction methods and machinery, relatively crude by today's standards, magnified the scope of the venture.

(From a booklet published by Public Service Company, **Serving Colorado for Fifty Years**, page 3. Furnished through the courtesy of Richard K. Weathers, supervisor of Boulder Hydro.)

112

Interior view of hydroelectric plant.

Nederland's fame as a mining town was gradually forgotten after the First World War. The annual summer migration of families who owned or rented cabins created a lesser fame — that of a summer resort. The town had always been noted for its streams and springs of pure water, its invigorating air and the charm of its location. Summer populations would sometimes rise to 1,500, while in winter less than 500 persons lived in town. Summer residents loved the fun of owning and renovating a deserted miner's cabin for carefree living. They enjoyed the tall tales of old-timers, the slow pace of the undemanding small community, the escape from city life. They hiked the mine-scarred mountains, and sometimes they just sat and watched the summer clouds drift by.

In the 1920s, the Model T Ford was enormously popular because it was inexpensive, versatile and easy to maintain. Henry Ford introduced the successful assembly-line method of production; mass production then enabled him to sell his Model T for $500. People of modest income could afford their own transportation.

My first memory of an automobile was my father's "T," which was our means of transportation. I remember vividly the canvas and isinglass side curtains my father would fasten in place when it rained.

Nederland entered my family history on June 28, 1922, when my parents bought a small frame house on the north hill from L.L. Yates and his wife Emma for the grand sum of $200. My parents and my brother and I then joined the summer migration of property owners who moved to the mountains for summertime living. We loved Nederland. Our home was in Denver the rest of the year. My father was equipment supervisor for Western Union, and he drove to Nederland every weekend.

We cleaned and painted and made improvements on the house, we carried our water by the bucketful from a central location on the hill, we had what my father called "air-cooled" toilet facilities, but we never felt deprived or thought of life in Nederland as work. Probably because there was lots of time left over for play, for exploring nearby places like the cemetery and the town dump. Hiking to various mines, often the Conger, was an exciting jaunt. We also had weekend trips via automobile when my father came to town, and we could take picnics to places like Eldora and Brainard Lake. One August, we hiked to the top of Arapaho Peak.

To my brother and me as young children, the most important places in Nederland were the post office, Fatty Mills picture show, and Tanner Bros. Grocery — all places where we were allowed to go unsupervised.

For about six weeks of the summer, a cousin came from Topeka, Kansas, to visit. Chauncey Lorenzo Sharpe was 12 days older than I, and my brother was 16 months older. We must have been extraordinarily compatible for I can't remember a single disagreement. When our cousin was in town, playtime always centered around mines. We built mines and dumps and roads and railroad track using treasures from the city dump for our imaginative purposes. Our cousin's life was permanently influenced by mines — he knew from childhood that he wanted mining to be his future. He never changed his mind. He went to the Colorado School of Mines for two years, then transferred to the Nevada School of Mines where he graduated. His first job was in Colorado, at Climax. From there he went to Canada, but never left mining as a career.

Our close neighbors on the north hill were families from Kansas who owned small frame houses similar to ours —the Resing family, the Cummings and Ruby Adams who was everyone's favorite. Henry Tanner, son of Ira Tanner of grocery store fame, lives in Longmont today. He remembers Ruby Adams very well. He says, "My mother used to hire me out to paint houses for her. When I finished, she always gave me a tip in cash. That was BIG MONEY to me." Ruby had no children of her own, but she knew how to show her appreciation. Probably she would be amused and delighted to be remembered years later for giving a tip.

Nederland as a resort town was well-known in a quiet way. Those who lived there year-round and people who discovered it for summer living adopted a guarded attitude, as if reluctant to tell a secret, perhaps fearing people would rush in again and spoil the serenity of their small town atmosphere. The smell of the pine trees, the sounds of rushing Middle Boulder Creek, the sight of water in the reservoir sparkling like diamonds in the sun, the forest pathways deep in pine needles leading to remote places where columbines and mariposa lilies could be found — all were charms known and guarded by those who lived in Nederland.

Homesteaders discovered these charms many years before tungsten made Nederland world-famous. Through the 1860s and into the 1870s, many farmers and ranchers were attracted to the rich meadowlands surrounding Nederland. More than 20 of these homesteaders are mentioned by name in Colorado histories. Alfred Tucker is one. The history of the Tucker Ranch includes the story of the first Arabian horses in Colorado, and later the Caribou Recording Studio. Each in turn brought fame once again to Nederland.

Alfred Tucker came from Illinois, settling in 1870 just west of Nederland along the road to Caribou. Years later, his son Tom purchased adjoining ranches, bringing together a large acreage, known today as Caribou Ranch. When Tom Tucker died, his sister Alice Moore bought the ranch.

From Alice Moore, Lynn W. Van Vleet purchased the 3,000-acre Tucker Ranch. Here he established the Lazy VV Ranch where the primary business was raising Hereford cattle. Arabian horses were brought into Colorado for the first time in May 1938 when Van Vleet purchased 29 purebred animals. Nederland was suddenly in the limelight again. Few people in the horse world believed that bringing desert horses into the high altitude of a mountain ranch could be successful.

Each horse had a lengthy and well-documented family tree. The star was Zarife, a purebred Arab stallion, foaled in Egypt in 1928 and purchased from Prince Mohamed Aly of Cairo. Another well regarded stallion was Rifage by the imported stallion Mirage. Van Vleet's group of brood mares and stallions became the talk of the western horse world. Experts knew the Arab stallion as the progenitor of the English Thoroughbred, the Morgan, the American Saddle-Horse, and virtually all other light horse breeds. Past ages have obscured the exact origin of the Arabian horse, but it has been well established that these horses have been scientifically bred pure for over 4,000 years.

Van Vleet reasoned that the same blood which made the Arab great on the desert would make him great anywhere, even in the rarefied air of the Rocky Mountains. In a 1944 interview with **Western Horseman**, he said:

I wanted to transplant this horse into totally different surroundings and revive — even intensify — the traits of courage, intelligence, resourcefulness and endurance which necessity and the experience of thousands of years of adversity in desert hardships bred into him. I wanted to bring the Arab into this mountain setting — which is as much the opposite of the desert as daylight is to dark — and substitute the rich diet of plentiful mountain meadows for the scarcity of desert lands, and substitute cooling, soothing mountain breezes for the hot winds of the desert.

Van Vleet's experiment worked beautifully — his Arabs thrived. They lived in lush mountain pastures instead of the hot sandy deserts of their homeland; they wore stock saddles instead of jewels; they were used for herding and roping cattle. Intelligent, responsive, strong and tireless, these magnificent animals learned their new trade quickly and well. With almost human understanding, they developed a talent for finding stray whiteface cattle in the timber.

Shortly after the arrival of the first Arabians, people would stop by the ranch hoping to see the horses. These visitors disrupted ranch routine to such a degree that Van Vleet, proud of his horses and eager to show them, opened his ranch to the public on Sundays. He had a show ring built. It was equipped with bleachers, a public address system and a special stand for photographers. Shows were produced each Sunday morning in summer from 1938 through 1950. The Arabians were put through the walk, trot and canter; some did memory and balancing tricks, others were shown in cutting exercises. Van Vleet presided at the microphone, describing his horses and explaining their performance. The highlight of these performances was a "charge" of five Arabian stallions mounted by cowboys in the colorful regalia of Bedouin warriors. According to **Empire Magazine** of July 2, 1967, Wayne Van Vleet remembered:

The shows took a lot of work, but we didn't mind. Everyone has a little showmanship in him, and the crowds were well-mannered and appreciative. It gave my Dad a chance to show what his Arabians could do, and he loved it. There was never any question about charging admission. Everyone who liked horses was welcome.

Opera stars from Central City always came over for the Sunday shows, Eleanor Steber and Regina Resnick to name but two. Many film personalities, Mae West and Gypsy Rose Lee, for example, were also visitors. Writers Ben Ames Williams, James Michener and Mari Sandoz came, were entertained and inspired. Each year more than 30,000 people saw the Arabs at the Lazy VV, and many more thousands saw them in color movies made by Warner Brothers and 20th Century Fox.

Through the years, Arabians from the Lazy VV Ranch were

shipped to 33 states and several foreign countries. In 1951, when his health no longer permitted him to spend long periods in high altitudes, Van Vleet sold the Lazy VV and moved the horses to their winter quarters near Boulder, Colorado. George Warren Barnes of Houston purchased the ranch and renamed it Caribou, a name which remains today.

What does the name Caribou mean today? Undoubtedly more widely recognized now because of the Caribou Recording Studio, the name still suggests "ghost town" or "silver mining" to many individuals. James W. Guercio bought the Caribou Ranch in 1971, and brought attention to Nederland by building a recording studio. It was one of the first "destination recording studios" in the United States, a welcome change for musicians working in big city studios of New York and Los Angeles.

Guercio — writer, musician and producer by profession — was only 28 years old and one of the most respected independent producers in the nation when he bought the Caribou Ranch. He is a man deeply interested in the concept of controlled land development. Much of his creative philosophy centers around his love for the land. Guercio, quoted in the Boulder **Daily Camera** of July 29, 1973, said:

I was fortunate through my success with records to be able to afford Caribou, so I feel I owe it to the land, to myself and everybody who values this country to try to preserve it. This is my whole dream. If I'm able to preserve 3,000 acres by building a recording studio in a barn, I want to do it.

The Caribou Recording Studio was unlike any other in its breathtakingly beautiful setting and its state-of-the-art facilities. Some of the most sophisticated recording equipment ever assembled in one studio was available there, and to musicians, it was a magical kingdom. They came not only to work but also to gain spiritual fulfillment in the peaceful mountain setting.

Some of the biggest names in music came to record — Stephen Stills, the Beach Boys, Chicago, Amy Grant, Dan Fogelberg, Chick Corea, and Michael Murphey, to name only a few. Elton John's album "Caribou" was named for the studio.

The Caribou Recording Studio was damaged by fire on March 2, 1985. The external structure has been rebuilt, but Caribou as a recording studio does not exist today. Guercio donated valuable recording equipment to the University of Colorado at Denver, including the 16-track sound board which he purchased from George Martin. The board, made for Martin, was used in producing many Beatle albums. Guercio said he believed the equipment would be better used at the college than if it were sold or traded.

Filmmaking and cable television are some of Jim Guercio's interests today. Film, he believes, can speak more eloquently than pop music to a generation that has great influence in our society.

1922 Ford Model T

Home owned by author's family, built on land that was originally part of Nathan Brown's homestead and Arapaho Peak.

Reservoir, circa 1920, and Tanner Bros. Grocery on Main Street, Nederland

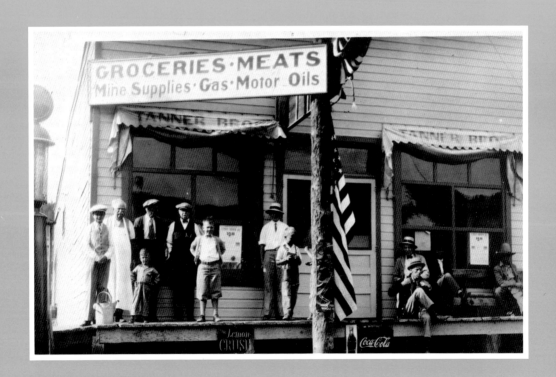

Road around Barker Reservoir, circa 1918

Zarife

Arabian Stallions in a Charge

# SCHOOL & CHURCH

## 10

   "A handsome structure has just been completed which will be used as a school house and church," reported the **Daily Rocky Mountain News** of September 18, 1872. From May to October was the school year in those early days, according to Geneva Meyring in **Nederland Then and Now.** In 1875 the one-room school had 30 to 35 students. Their teacher was "B.T. Napier, a handsome young man from Missouri." With older girls, noted Meyring, he was a "special favorite."

   Despite the vicissitudes of life in Nederland, the school was always a vital institution. Even in 1889 when only seven families lived in town, Nederland had a school.

   A second schoolhouse with two rooms was built in 1907. Both buildings were used until a fire in 1910 destroyed the new one. Immediately, residents of Nederland approved rebuilding, this time a four-room school which was ready for use the next year. In 1916, this building was enlarged to six rooms. In 1921, the curriculum was expanded to include all four years of high school.

Works Progress Administration funds and a 1936 bond issue approved by voters made possible the next change. Three more classrooms, a science room, library and gymnasium were added. The **W.P.A. Worker** of March 1937 described the addition as a stone annex that enlarged Nederland School to more than twice its former size. The publication enumerated the new rooms and added "an auditorium and other modern facilities" not mentioned by Meyring.

Today the buildings on the north side of town are used for elementary grades only. Nederland Junior Senior High School, opened in 1971, is located southwest of town on the road to Eldora. Nederland's present school system is incorporated in Boulder Valley School District and enrolls students from outlying areas within a 12-mile radius of town.

The future of education in Nederland looks promising. The town will have a new elementary school and the Junior Senior High School will have a new gym and science laboratory. Voters approved a school bond issue on December 6, 1988, although only a year earlier a similar school bond, strongly supported by Nederland, was turned down by a majority of Boulder County voters.

The Nederland area community, experiencing steady

growth in recent years, has struggled with severe overcrowding of school facilities. The new school for elementary grades and new facilities for the Junior Senior High School are basic needs. Architectural drawings for Nederland Elementary School have been made by NBBB Architects in Boulder, the building site has been chosen, and bidding processes for construction will take place in the near future. Nederland people look forward to these changes.

Schoolhouse in Nederland, 1872

Nederland Junior Senior High School, 1988

Architectural drawing for Nederland Elementary School

(Permission to photograph given by Phil Atchison of Boulder Valley School District.)

Pine-shaded St. Rita's Catholic Church started out as a rustic log chapel half the size of the present church. The old Antlers Hotel, purchased by the Catholic Daughters of America in 1932, was converted to a summer camp for girls, and the chapel was built in 1935 especially for the campers. The chapel stood just east of the old hotel. Except for a few summers during the Second World War, the camp was open every summer for more than 20 years. In 1954 the Daughters bought another camp and closed the one at Nederland. By 1961, the two-story frame building, once Nederland's finest hotel, was in a state of disrepair and was torn down. The original chapel of St. Rita was enlarged to create the church standing today on the hill called Montrita.

The "Little Brown Church," Nederland Community Presbyterian, was officially organized on August 19, 1912, with a membership of 12. This picturesque little frame building made its appearance in 1915 through the efforts of townspeople who contributed money and long hours of work to the project. Adorning the top of the structure is a small tower containing an old fire bell which once was the property of the Boulder Fire Department. Members say there is no thrill like hearing the old bell ring out in the crystal-clear air on Sunday mornings.

Calvary Chapel had its beginning in 1979 as many small churches do, as a Bible study group. With only two couples at first, their numbers soon increased to about 25, and then it was no longer convenient to meet in private homes. They met for about one year in the school auditorium. When an A-frame became available, the group decided to buy it — the building was affordable, exactly the amount of money being kept in savings for construction of a church. Later, a new sanctuary was built on the east side of the A-frame, nearly doubling the size of the original church.

# RECENT TIMES

## 11

Communities everywhere face problems that arise with change. The social and political ferment of the sixties in America spilled over into Nederland in the late 1960s and early 1970s. The influx of hippies coming into town resulted in some very undesirable media attention. Nederland was described at various times as a battle zone, with war going on between hippies and old-timers. According to newspaper accounts, violence characterized the era. Brawls, stabbings and heavy drug use gave the town a bad reputation. The times were distressing for Nederland, but troublemakers in the counterculture eventually moved on; by 1975, most problems attributed to them had faded from newspaper front pages.

A new issue confronted the town in 1981 — a proposal to annex 300 acres of land for residential development. Opinion was divided between those who believed the annexation could mean prosperity for Nederland and those who opposed the idea of swift and sprawling expansion, wanting to retain the town's secluded character.

Today, media attention is again focused on Nederland. Opposing groups of citizens, with their differing visions of progress, are trying to resolve some serious matters. Early in December 1988, a group of angry citizens formed a committee to recall the mayor. News of their action was reported in Nederland's weekly newspaper, **The Mountain-Ear**, December 8, 1988. Each week thereafter through the month of December and into part of January 1989, new developments in the recall movement made front-page news in the Nederland newspaper. Inevitably, the recall campaign was given coverage in other Colorado newspapers.

In 1989, Kevin McCullen of the **Rocky Mountain News** made several reports on the progress of Nederland's recall issue. On March 10, 1989, McCullen quoted Town Manager Dave Clyne who said, "It's time to talk issues now, and are we taking the right direction with the town? Does Nederland want a town park, boating on Barker Reservoir, construction of trails?" Clyne welcomed the prospect of a recall election. Nederland people could "leap at this recall" if they opposed changes being made, or vote against it if they thought the mayor was doing a good job. An election could settle the controversies.

Petitions to recall the mayor were eventually received by Town Clerk Alisa Lewis, and a recall election was set for April 25, 1989. On April 26, 1989, Boulder's newspaper, the

**Daily Camera**, announced "NEDERLAND OFFICIALS RETAIN SEATS." The recall election attracted a record turnout of voters, and when the defeat was announced, wrote Margie McAllister, "the crowd howled with pleasure and burst into applause." Then the five trustees "donned Groucho Marx glasses with fake furry eyebrows and mustaches" to mimic Mayor Art Yoetis' looks and to celebrate his victory.

Many townspeople feel they have been wronged by negative press in the past. But apparently Nederland has never been permanently damaged by such publicity. People continue to choose the community for their homes. Roger Cornell and his wife, Karen, chose Nederland in 1977. They bought property "on the ridge above town," wrote Barbara Lawlor in **The Mountain-Ear** December 19, 1988, and built their home. Today the Cornells are a family with two children. Roger Cornell is a member of the town board of trustees as well as a member of Nederland's planning commission. Both jobs are unpaid. As their predecessors gave to this mountain community many years ago, Roger and Karen give gladly and freely to theirs.

Catherine Horowitz is another person who likes having a home base in Nederland. When Catherine and her husband, Stuart, came back from Japan in 1979 and arrived in Boulder, it was summer and Boulder was hot. In an interview August 10, 1988, Catherine said, "Our friends knew we were looking for a place to live and told us we wouldn't want to live in Nederland." They came up to look, however, and "Nederland appealed," declared Catherine. "We bought property in Nederland and have never regretted it."

Rob Schneider was Nederland's hard-working president of the Chamber of Commerce, doing shovel work at the Visitors Center one summer day in 1988. He expressed his optimism and interest in the town by saying, "Sooner or later, First Street will be the arts and crafts center of Nederland." Schneider also believes that "the town's younger generation will build something for senior citizens, perhaps a greenhouse where they could work and raise flowers to sell to various business establishments."

The Colorado Tourism Board awarded Rob Schneider "top honor for volunteer achievement this year," reported the **Mountain-Ear** on April 13, 1989. Other individuals and organizations throughout Colorado were considered for the honor. Schneider was chosen because his achievements were "outstanding examples of contributions to tourism in Colorado."

In recent years, Nederland leaders have actively searched for ways to revitalize the town and generate tourist dollars. Several interesting proposals by students attending Colorado University at Denver were submitted in the spring of 1984.

Originally the students' work was to take a week's time and focus on the downtown section around Five Points, the intersection where five streets converge. Their assignment was simply to come up with a few sketches to illustrate ideas they thought could make improvements. Interest grew and the project expanded to include the whole town, said Professor Lauri MacMillan Johnson, the students' advisor at the College of Design and Planning. Proposals were rendered in color in beautifully finished architectural drawings.

"The Stage" was one theme proposed, and the ideas it contained were consistent with Nederland's past history as a mining center. An old-time western stagecoach was to be the focal point. Stagecoach runs to Blackhawk, Caribou, Ward and Lake Eldora were planned. Stops along the way at scenic points and places of historical interest were suggested.

A detailed study was presented to the Nederland Chamber of Commerce. It was a long-range plan in three phases, designed to focus on cultural, historic, artistic and natural resources already existing. These students saw the enthusiasm of Nederland residents as one of the town's natural resources.

Two improvements suggested — a tourist information center and a trail system along Middle Boulder Creek — now exist as finished projects in Nederland. Both are a source of pride to the town and a tribute to the enthusiasm and hard work of local people and some University of Colorado at Denver students.

"This past year," wrote John Gunn in **Peak to Peak Magazine** (September/October 1988), "an ad hoc citizens' group" met regularly to consider the future of Nederland. These planners want to make their town attractive to tourists without changing the small town atmosphere that local people love and enjoy. Town planners ask: Why do people visit Nederland? They believe visitors have a nostalgia for the past and want to see qualities no longer existing in their own communities. Nederland, planners conclude, needs a master plan. The town has a rich and interesting past, and future development requires wise planning.

Making East First Street a one-way thoroughfare with wide board sidewalks reminiscent of early-day Nederland is being considered. Burying telephone and power lines, paving the street, neatly painting and trimming fronts of buildings along each side, installing flower boxes and benches, planting trees — all are changes that are not financially impossible for the town.

Nederland has already made progress with the completion of three projects: a covered pedestrian bridge, a tourist information center and a walking trail along Middle Boulder Creek.

The roofed bridge for pedestrians, located just east of the highway bridge over Middle Boulder Creek, leads into the walking trail. To walk across this bridge is to appreciate the work of Rob Schneider who designed and engineered its construction when he was president of Nederland's Chamber of Commerce. Schneider said he and his three sons built the bridge.

The tourist center is located in a well-chosen site for visitor convenience and visibility, and there is parking nearby. A grand opening celebration took place on August 26, 1988. Chuck Webb, president of Nederland National Bank, said main financial contributors were Public Service, Mountain Bell, RTD, the County of Boulder, the Town of Nederland and the Nederland Chamber of Commerce.

The walking trail along Middle Boulder Creek was also completed in 1988, the work of volunteers. The trail begins at the covered bridge, follows Middle Boulder Creek to the reservoir, crosses the weir bridge and continues along the west edge of Barker Reservoir. Picnic tables, small charcoal grills and trash receptacles are in place at several areas along the pathway.

Tom Hendricks and Mike Savage donated significant amounts of time and hard work to Nederland's trail system and were given special recognition by the Town of Nederland. Town officials presented both men with Golden Nugget Awards. Hendricks is president of Cross Mine in

Caribou, and Savage, an apprentice miner, works with him. In addition to his volunteer work on the trail, Hendricks gave the Visitors Center "silver ore and an ore bucket," reported **The Mountain-Ear** of August 18, 1988.

"Beginning in the late fall of 1987, Barker Reservoir was drained empty," said Skip Arnold from Public Service Company in Boulder. "We probably won't see this low-water stage again for some years, although it won't be as many as 17. They waited too long this time" to do maintenance work on the 10 hydraulically operated gates in Barker Dam.

The photograph on page 150 was taken one cold day in early April 1988. The raised earthen pathway receding toward the dam is the grade of a temporary railroad, built when Barker Dam was being constructed in the early 1900s. After being submerged in the waters of the reservoir for 78 years, it is still unmistakable.

The sight of the empty reservoir was shocking. Tons of ice lining the sides of the empty reservoir were collapsing under their own weight as water drained out. This left an eerie calcified residue on the banks.

We walked toward the dam that freezing day in April wondering how long it takes for the reservoir to fill. One season? Two? From our lake-bottom view, I imagined Middle Boulder Creek could never fill that huge expanse in one season.

"Water spilled for about one month, beginning toward the

end of June," said Arnold. "Usually water spills over the dam about the second week of May and spills for about one month. This year (1988) it was later."

Middle Boulder Creek is mightier than it looks.

End of the line!

Coach and four to Nederland

Visitors Center in Nederland

Barker Reservoir at low-water stage

Photograph of the east face of the dam taken around the end of June 1988 shows the spillway, the lake level as water spilled over the top, and the aged yet still structurally sound concrete work that was completed in 1910.

The two-story home Wesley Hetzer built in 1870 stands in the foreground of this picture. This photograph is thought to have been made in 1872, one of the earliest known pictures of Nederland. The Hetzer family and their descendents were a highly respected pioneer group, prominent in the social and political life of the town. "From the time they came," wrote historian Geneva Meyring, "they gave fully and freely to community life."

Fate was kind to the Hetzer family home as compared with many original buildings in town. Milt Moore learned that the house was to be used in a fire drill, set on fire, and totally demolished. He bought it for one dollar and moved it into a residential development on the south side of Barker Reservoir. It stands today at 49 Blue Spruce Drive, the 118-year-old beautifully restored home of John and Alisa Lewis.

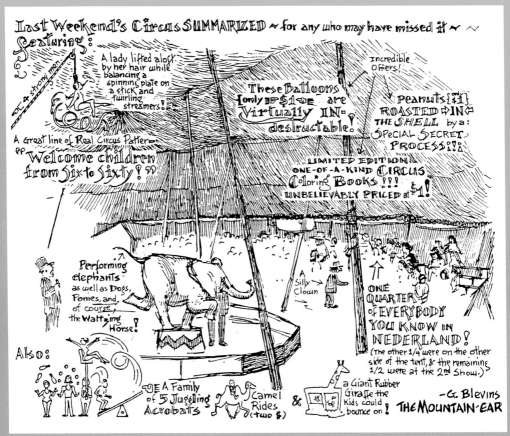

George Blevins' drawing speaks eloquently for the circus that came to town on Saturday, July 30, 1988.

**Fred the Town Cat.**
Born behind a jukebox
in a local eatery during
the heyday of the Hippie
Invasion, Fred is fed &
cared for by donations
from folks who respect
his right to live as he
chooses. - No one knows
where he spends his nights.

The story of this furry talk-of-the-town character, sketched by George Blevins, cannot be left out of Nederland's history.

# INDEX

# IMAGE CREDITS

Page 33: **Silver bromide print** by S. Becker

Page 34: **Silver bromide print** by S. Becker

Page 35: **Silver bromide print** by S. Becker

Page 36: **Second generation silver print,** First Federal Bank Collection

Page 37: **Pen and ink drawing** by Carl Wulsten, **The Great Divide Magazine**

Page 38: **Silver bromide print** by S. Becker

Page 47: **Original watercolor** by Tom Berger WPA

Page 48: **Silver print,** Carnegie Branch Library for Local History

Page 49: **Silver print,** Carnegie Branch Library for Local History

Page 50: **Original charcoal drawing** by George Blevins

Page 51: **Silver bromide print** by S. Becker

Page 52: **Chromolithograph** by William Henry Jackson

Page 53: **Silver bromide print** by S. Becker

Page 54: **Resin-coated print,** Eldora Ski Resort

Page 64: **Silver bromide print** by S. Becker

Page 65: **Silver bromide print** by S. Becker

Page 66: **Silver bromide print** by S. Becker

Page 67: **Original watercolor** by Tom Berger WPA

Page 68: **Second generation silver print,** First Federal Bank Collection

Page 69: **Pen and ink drawing with colored pencil,** Colorado School of Mines, Map Archives

Page 70: **Pen and ink drawing with colored pencil,** Colorado School of Mines, Map Archives

Page 71: **Second generation silver print,** Denver Public Library, Western History Department

Page 72: **Second generation silver print,** First Federal Bank Collection

Page 73: **Second generation silver print,** Colorado Historical Society

Page 74: **Silver bromide print** by S. Becker

Page 78: **Original graphite drawing** by John Sorbie

Page 79: **Original watercolor** by Tom Berger WPA

Page 80: **Original pencil drawing** by George Blevins

Page 81: **Original watercolor** by Tom Berger WPA

Page 92: **Second generation silver print,** First Federal Bank Collection

Page 93: **Second generation silver print,** First Federal Bank Collection

Page 94: **Color lithograph,** Colorado Historical Society

Page 95: **Original graphite drawing** by John Sorbie

Page 96: **Second generation silver print,** First Federal Bank Collection

Page 97: **Silver print,** author's collection

Page 98: **Silver bromide print** by S. Becker

Page 99: **Letterpress print,** Jimmy Keith Collection

Page 100: **Second generation silver print,** First Federal Bank Collection

Page 101: **Second generation silver print,** First Federal Bank Collection

Page 107: **1920s postcard,** author's collection

Page 108: **Print from a glass plate negative** by William Henry Jackson

Page 109: **Original graphite drawing** by John Sorbie

Page 110: **Silver bromide print** by S. Becker

Page 111: **Second generation silver print,** Jimmy Keith Collection

Page 112: **Original pencil drawing** by George Blevins

Page 113: **Silver bromide print** by S. Becker

Page 124: **Original graphite drawing** by John Sorbie

Page 125 top: **Silver print,** author's collection

Page 125 bottom: **Silver print,** author's collection

Page 126 top: **Silver print,** author's collection

Page 126 bottom: **Silver print,** Henry Tanner Collection

Page 127: **Sepia-toned silver print,** author's collection

Page 128: **Silver print,** Van Vleet Collection

Page 129: **Silver print,** Van Vleet Collection

Page 134: **Second generation silver print,** Carnegie Branch Library for Local History

Page 135: **Silver bromide print** by S. Becker

Page 136: **Architectural rendering,** Boulder Valley Public Schools

Page 137: **Silver bromide print** by S. Becker

Page 138 top: **1920s postcard,** author's collection

Page 138 bottom: **Silver bromide print** by S. Becker

Page 147: **Original watercolor** by Tom Berger WPA

Page 148: **Original watercolor** by Tom Berger WPA

Page 149: **Silver bromide print** by S. Becker

Page 150: **Silver bromide print** by S. Becker

Page 151: **Silver bromide print** by S. Becker

Page 152: **Second generation silver print,** Colorado Historical Society

Page 153: **Silver bromide print** by S. Becker

Page 154: **Original pen and ink drawing** by George Blevins

Page 155: **Original pen and ink drawing** by George Blevins

Note: **WPA** added to Tom Berger's name indicates his membership in the prestigious international organization, the Whiskey Painters of America.

# MORE READING

Books:

Bixby, A., et al. **History of Clear Creek and Boulder Valleys, Colorado.** Chicago: O.L. Baskin & Company, 1880.

Crossen, Forest. **The Switzerland Trail of America.** Fort Collins: Robinson Press, Inc., 1978.

Jackson, Clarence S. **Picture Maker of the Old West.** New York: Bonanza Books, no publishing date listed.

Kemp, Donald. **Silver, Gold and Black Iron.** Denver: Sage Books, 1960.

Meyring, Geneva. **Nederland Then and Now.** Privately printed, 1941.

Noel, Thomas J. **Colorado Catholicism, 1857 to 1988.** Scheduled for publication by University Press of Colorado, November 1989.

Pettem, Silvia. **Red Rocks to Riches.** Denver: Stonehenge Books, 1980.

Smith, Duane A. **Silver Saga.** Boulder: Pruett Publishing Company, 1974.

Wallihan, S.S. and T.O. Bigney (eds.). **The Rocky Mountain Directory and Colorado Gazetteer for 1871.** Denver: S.S. Wallihan and Company, 1870.

**Westerners Brand Book, 1947.** Denver: The Artcraft Press, 1949.

**Westerners Brand Book, 1968.** Boulder: Johnson Publishing Company, 1969.

Wolle, Muriel S. **Stampede to Timberline.** Denver: The Artcraft Press, 1952.

**W.P.A. Guide to 1930 Colorado.** Introduction by Thomas J. Noel. Topeka: University Press of Kansas, 1987.

Journals:

**Mining in Boulder County, Colorado.** Boulder: The Boulder County Metal Mining Association, August 2, 1915.

**The Mining Industry and Tradesman.** W. C. Wynkoop, ed. Denver: The Mining Industry Publishing Company, June 23, 1892.

Unpublished material:

Interview with Samuel P. Conger. **Sam Conger, Mineral and Mine Finder.** Mss IX-15. Denver: Colorado State Historical Society, October 15, 1921.

# T H A N K S

## My Sincere Thanks To Nederland People Who Showed Interest In This Project And Took Time Out To Be Helpful

George Blevins
Glenna and Tom Carline
Karen Cox
Celeste Haselwood
Ruby Jackson
Kay and Stuart Horowitz

Alisa and John Lewis
Rob Schneider
Irene Smith
Jack Snyder
Bob Stouffer
Chuck Webb

## Thanks To Others, Not Local People

Lois Anderton, Boulder
Phil Atchison, Denver
Tom Hendricks, Caribou
Donna Hudgel, Louisville
Rose and John Jackson, Tungsten

James E. Miller, Longmont
Carol Rinderknecht, Eldora
Allan B. Rogers, Boulder
Henry Tanner, Longmont
Richard K. Weathers, Boulder

## Still Others Who Helped In Significant Ways

Ken Atkinson
Dan Becker
Beverly Breshears
Cec Burkhardt
Bud Collier

Doris Frick
Jim Guercio
Janet Heritage
Susan Miller
Wayne Van Vleet

## Tom Noel And Silvia Pettem Were My Professional Advisors. They Gave Generously Of Their Knowledge On Numerous Occasions.

Original ideas and graphic art by Scott Becker. Personal support by Con Becker and Susan Miller. Typeset by Linda Bertelson. Printed by Richard Shorey. Published by SCOTT BECKER PRESS.

Author's note: With appreciation, I want to acknowledge having used, stolen or plagiarized ideas from Chris O'Shea, Sara Davidson, Marjorie Barrett, Theodore Roszak and Don F. Amen.

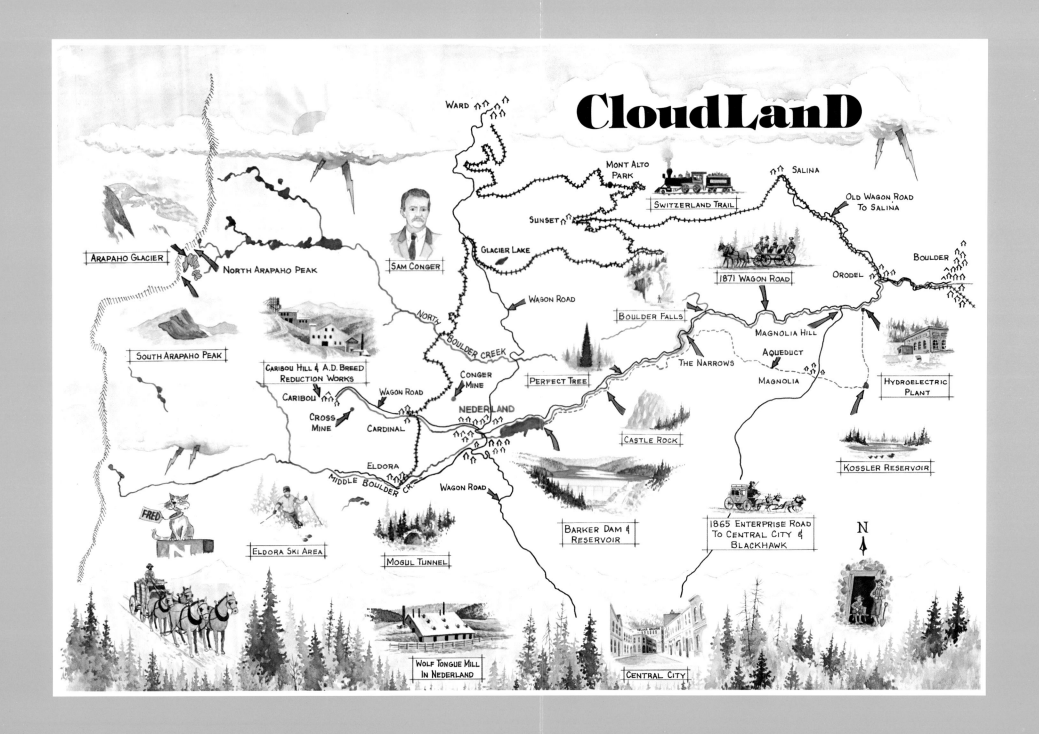

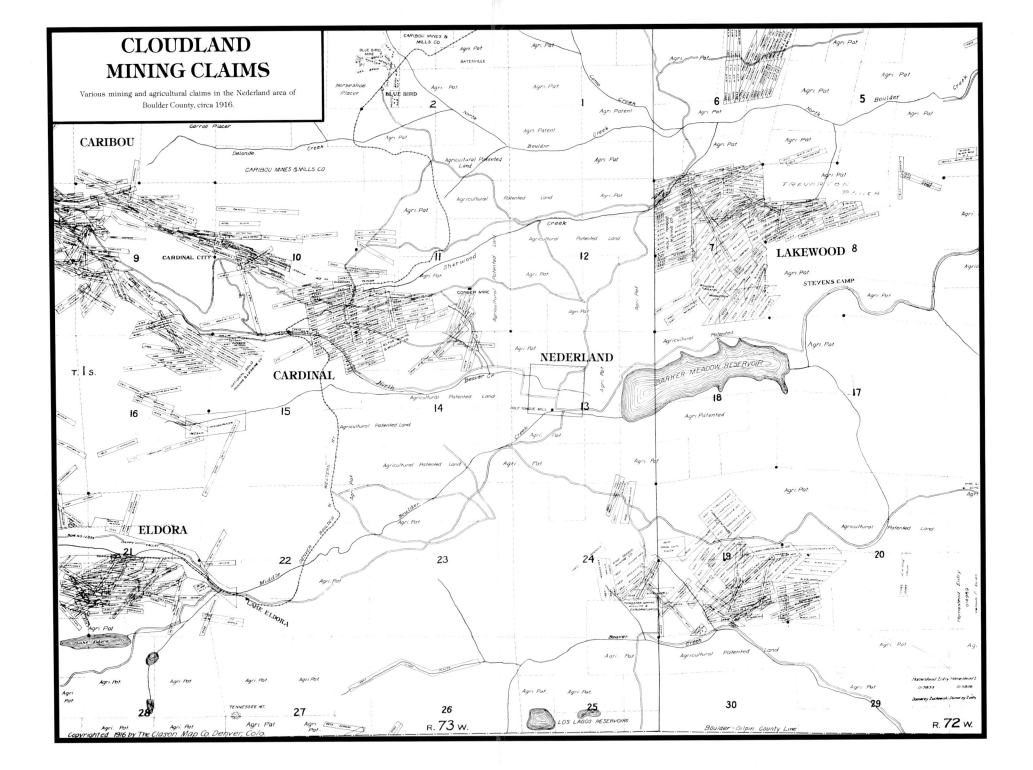

# CLOUDLAND MINING CLAIMS

Various mining and agricultural claims in the Nederland area of Boulder County, circa 1916.

Copyrighted 1916 by The Clason Map Co. Denver, Colo.